"This book offers a concise yet rich overview of Ratzinger's profound vision of Christian faith. I have no doubt that Fr. Cardó's work will help many of the faithful grow in their understanding of what it means to believe. It will also give them the insights needed to grow stronger in their faith and live it out in a society that is increasingly dismissive of it. I recommend this timely and accessible book to anyone who wants to live an intelligent faith with conviction in the modern world."

> MATTHEW RAMAGE
> Benedictine College
> Author of *The Experiment of Faith*

"More than anything else, we need a renewed encounter with the person of Jesus Christ and, through faith in him, communion within the divine life of the Trinity. Fr. Daniel Cardó focuses us on this burning necessity, drawing upon the rich thought of Joseph Ratzinger. In an age bound by the visible, yet still thirsting for the infinite, there is nothing more important for both the Church and society than strengthening our belief in God and allowing him to be the center of all we do. I commend Fr. Cardó for making Ratzinger's insights more accessible, pointing us back to the centrality of faith, the only path to true freedom."

> MOST REV. SAMUEL J. AQUILA
> Archbishop of Denver

"At 1 Peter 3:15 we find the words, 'Always be prepared to make a defense to any one who calls you to account for the hope that is in you.' In this work one can read the defenses of Joseph Ratzinger, who is not just another big-name theologian, but *the* theologian of our time, the way that Newman was the theologian of the nineteenth century. In this 'back to the fourteenth century' decade of clerical corruption, something like the plague, and rampant nominalism, Fr. Cardó's reflection on Ratzinger's understanding of faith is a very consoling and edifying contribution to Emmaus Academic."

TRACEY ROWLAND
University of Notre Dame (Australia)

"As we witness a global recalibration and rebalancing, Fr. Cardó places in our hands a refreshingly lucid summary of Joseph Ratzinger's understanding of faith to carry us through the twenty-first century. Far from anthropocentric, Christian faith is personal and Christ-centered: '*Cor ad cor loquitur*' (St. John Henry Newman). Fr. Cardó shows that faith is an entrusting of the human self to Christ in the mind of Ratzinger. Highly recommended."

FR. EMERY DE GAÁL
University of Saint Mary of the Lake,
Mundelein Seminary

What Does it Mean to Believe?

What Does it Mean to Believe?

FAITH IN THE THOUGHT OF JOSEPH RATZINGER

FR. DANIEL CARDÓ

Steubenville, Ohio
www.emmausacademic.com

EMMAUS
ACADEMIC

Steubenville, Ohio
www.emmausacademic.com
A Division of The St. Paul Center for Biblical Theology
Editor-in-Chief: Scott Hahn
1468 Parkview Circle
Steubenville, Ohio 43952

© 2020 Daniel Cardó
All rights reserved. 2020
Printed in the United States of America

Library of Congress Cataloging-in-Publication Data Applied For
ISBN: 978-1-64585-041-0 (hc)

Unless otherwise noted, Scripture quotations are taken from The Revised Standard Version Second Catholic Edition (Ignatius Edition) Copyright © 2006 by the Division of Christian Education of the National Council of the Churches of Christ in the United States of America. Used by permission. All rights reserved.

Excerpts from the Catechism of the Catholic Church, second edition, copyright © 2000, Libreria Editrice Vaticana—United States Conference of Catholic Bishops, Washington, D.C. Noted as "CCC" in the text.

Cover design and layout by Emily Demary
Cover image: Joseph Ratzinger. Photo by Levan Ramishvili.

To Pope Emeritus Benedict XVI, with filial gratitude.

To believe is none other than, in the obscurity of the world, to touch the hand of God and thus, in silence, to hear the Word, to see Love.

(Joseph Ratzinger—Benedict XVI)

Table of Contents

Foreword by Cardinal Gerhard L. Müller..........xi
Acknowledgments...xv
Introduction..1

I. Believing in the Context of the
Contemporary World....................................13
    1. Doubt and Faith: The Perennial
        Challenge of Believing......................14
    2. The Contemporary Form of
        the Crisis of Faith.............................19

II. Faith as Gift Given and
Gift Received..35
    1. Faith as a Gift Given.........................35
    2. Christian Faith as a Gift
        Received...38

III. Faith as an Act..53
    1. Faith as a Personal Act.....................53
    2. Faith as an Integral Act...................69
    3. Faith as an Ecclesial Act..................85

Afterword..99
Bibliography...101
Index..109

Foreword

We live in a time of deep changes and crises. Although in many ways the advances made in the past decades in the areas of technology and communication are truly revolutionary and have opened hitherto unthinkable possibilities for connection and progress, the isolation and lack of stable relationships cast a shadow of doubt over the otherwise epic achievements of human ingenuity. It is true that, in the big picture, there are fewer wars and, statistically speaking, fewer people dying of hunger than in earlier centuries. But real injustice still causes pain and death for too many people; instability looms over previously stable societies; and violence appears in unexpected ways. In the political realm, polarization makes honest debate at times virtually impossible. And in the world of moral values, what was universally sacred some years ago is now a matter of personal preference.

This instability is also present in the life of the Church. Along with many other signs of malaise, doctrinal confusion and a certain form of polarization appear as critical challenges for the life and mission of the Church. How can the Church of Christ proclaim the Good News if there are so many significant disagreements about fundamental aspects of our faith and morals?

In times of insecurity, a common temptation is that of pragmatism. We are aware that we need answers, and so we try to find the right measures to fix the problem. And yet we know that we must go deeper than that. A crisis, as a time of profound change, is also a possibility for growth. But, for this to happen, we need to go to the roots of the situation. The questions cannot be only about practical decisions, but about the meaning of humanity, about our origin and purpose. Because of this, we need to seek the truth of our life; because of this, we need to ask the question about God.

Faith, far from being an accessory reality for those who can afford the luxury of lofty thoughts, is a necessary endeavor, yesterday, today, and tomorrow. There is in reality nothing more important, and nothing more urgent than faith. For, if God is real, if He can be known, if our life can be accompanied and strengthened by Him, then everything changes. Reflecting on faith is a matter of the utmost importance.

This is true not only in terms of what we believe in; also, and perhaps even first, in terms of what it means to believe. What happens when we say that we believe in God? Can a human person of our pluralist society believe in *one* God? Is faith only a sentimental matter? Is faith opposed to reason? Can we encounter God as a person?

Joseph Ratzinger—Pope Benedict XVI (2005–2013), one of the truly great theologians of our age, has offered insightful and relevant contributions to our understanding of faith. As we have come to expect from him, the depths and intricacies of the truths explored are conveyed with transparent strength, rooted in his extraordinary knowledge and, even more, in his extraordinary love of God and reverence for the human heart.

In the preface to the first volume of his *Collected Works*—which Benedict XVI entrusted to me as editor—he talked about what has been the core of his long and prolific intellectual work: "I wanted above all to go to the heart of the question: Why do we believe?"

Father Cardó's book is a welcome contribution that will help many people to benefit from the richness of Ratzinger's thoughts on faith. It comes at a good moment, when in the midst of so much turbulence we need to go more than ever to the roots of our life, and face the challenge of believing in today's world.

This volume chooses rightly to begin the review of Ratzinger's many works by going to one of the most famous books published by the Pope Emeritus: *Introduction to Christianity*, which was published just over fifty years ago. That influential volume offers a compelling meditation on the Creed, but before that, it invites the reader—or the hearer, as the book is the transcript of conferences given at the University of Tübingen—to reflect on what it means for a human being to believe, and to believe today, with the particular challenges of our times. From there, Father Cardó takes us on a journey in which he connects several other works by Joseph Ratzinger, presenting an organic overview of the thoughts of Joseph Ratzinger on the act of believing.

The reading of this brief work can be a fruitful exercise in acquiring familiarity with the theology of faith developed by Joseph Ratzinger, a theology that, while rich and relevant, was not written in the manner of a manual. Faith is present in a significant number of the Pope Emeritus' works, and is perhaps best understood as one of the transversal axes of his overall theological view.

I believe and hope that the reading of this book will bring another fruit: an increased desire to go directly to the works of Joseph Ratzinger, organized now in the sixteen volumes of his *Collected Works*.

When difficult questions arise about serious situations in the Church and in the world, when insecurity and confusion become all too present in the life of believers and unbelievers alike, we need to pause from our hectic busyness and seek the truth.

Joseph Ratzinger's great master, St. Augustine, said it simply and beautifully: "What does our soul desire more passionately than truth—*Quid enim fortius desiderat anima quam veritatem?*" (*In Ioannis* 26, 5).

I wish this book a wide readership, so that amidst crises and changes we can all desire the truth with ever greater passion, and thus rediscover the gift and adventure of faith.

Rome, January 31, 2019
Cardinal Gerhard L. Müller

Acknowledgments

I WOULD LIKE TO OFFER a word of gratitude to those who have helped me in the process of writing, translating, and adapting this book, based on an earlier work published by the University of Navarre in Spain (EUNSA) in 2013. To Angie Woods, Vladimir Mauricio Pérez, Geraldine Kelley, Mary Gillum, and Caroline Chihoski: know of my gratitude for your contribution. In the midst of the demands of parish life and teaching, even a short volume like this could not exist without the generosity and talent of good friends.

Needless to say, I humbly thank Joseph Ratzinger—Pope Emeritus Benedict XVI—for his testimony and teachings on the faith; I hope that many can drink from the font of his legacy. I also thank Scott Hahn, Chris Erickson, and Daniel Seseske at Emmaus Academic for their professional and faithful service to the Church. Finally, I would like to thank my parents, and my parishioners at Holy Name Parish, who day by day choose to believe in the midst of so many challenges, constantly teaching me how to renew my faith.

Introduction

A BOOK ON FAITH?
A BOOK ON RATZINGER?

These two questions are important; in fact, the success of this volume depends upon answering them adequately. Allow me to begin with two personal experiences.

I will start with the second question. In May 2017, I had the unique joy of meeting with Joseph Ratzinger. Words can hardly express what that meant for me. The first book I read at the beginning of my priestly formation was his *The God of Jesus Christ*. I continued to read his works with great fruit. One of the happiest days of my life was April 19, 2005, when the name *Iosephum Sanctae Romanae Ecclesiae Cardinalem Ratzinger* resounded from the loggia announcing his election as Successor of Peter. One of the strangest days of my life was February 11, 2013, when a friend called from Rome before dawn with the news of Benedict XVI's resignation.

Even after Benedict became Pope Emeritus, I continued to read his works, not only as great sources of theological information, but especially as particularly insightful guidelines for the right direction of my own spiritual, pastoral, and academic life. So, the long-awaited time to meet in person with this doctor and modern Father of the Church was, as you can imagine, a highlight in my life.

It was a lovely spring evening when, after praying the Holy Rosary with his secretary Archbishop Gänswein, he stood up to wait for his visit. What impressed me the most was his simplicity: one of the brightest intellects in the world, the accomplished author of dozens of books and hundreds of articles, and the only bearer of the title Pope Emeritus, had no agenda and no other interest than hearing about me. He seemed very, very frail, but his mind was lucid. While clearly not a "chatter," he never stopped asking questions, with particular interest in academic topics, including the number of students I was teaching at that time (which I was not able to answer accurately!). On that occasion, I gave him the first Spanish edition of this book.

In the course of our conversation, as I was concentrating on trying to speak Italian properly, this thought came to me: "You are talking with Benedict. Look at him. Don't worry about your grammar." And so I did: I looked at his eyes and enjoyed the meeting. And I saw deep goodness, honest humility, and profound peace. As he was picked up in a little cart, I noticed that Archbishop Gänswein had to carry him and sit him in the cart. He could barely walk.

Going back to the noisy streets of Rome, I was taken by the thought that I had met not only what you could call my "academic hero," but, perhaps, a living saint: someone who, as his namesake St. Benedict wrote, placed nothing before the love of Christ. I also had the distinct impression of having encountered one of those few minds that will influence the Church and the world for centuries to come. His simplicity almost hides his erudition. How true it is what his friend, the late Cardinal Meisner said of him: "He is as intelligent as twelve professors, and as devout as a First Communion child."

I was grateful for meeting, I might say, the last of a special generation of towering figures that decisively marked the life of the Church in the twentieth and twenty-first centuries. Independent of intellectual affinities, the name Ratzinger is the last of an illustrious list: Guardini, de Lubac, Rahner, von Balthasar, Daniélou, and a few others. To be sure, there are great theologians working in the Church today, people with great culture and experience. But it is not easy to find a name that could join that list of not only accomplished authors, but of wise and visionary, integral and prophetic, faithful and synthetic souls. Joseph Ratzinger might be the last of a generation.

This is why it makes sense to write another book on Joseph Ratzinger: to help, in some way, to appreciate the decisive contribution of a man of his stature, whose memory is very much alive, whose legacy is still far from being fully appreciated, and whose figure remains involved in the mystery of a spiritually fruitful yet very complicated pontificate.

Now, why another book on faith? The simple answer: because it is not always easy to believe.

I grew up in an environment in which faith was a given. Believing in God was as natural as eating and breathing. How I treasure the memory of those

Sunday Masses in the beautiful colonial churches of Lima, followed by a wonderful lunch with my parents and siblings. How I miss believing together with them. How I hope faith will grow again for all.

However, while faith was not a problem, I still had to encounter Jesus Christ as a person and intentionally choose to follow Him. The moment came as I was finishing high school. Then, after encountering Him in a profoundly personal way, I heard his call to the priesthood. Faith then was not simply a self-evident proposition, it was a passion: not an immature fixation, but a real choice. It was friendship, discipleship, and a commitment to the apostolate. My years in formation were, while not always easy, a treasured and beautiful experience of getting to know and love Jesus Christ more deeply. Then came my perpetual promises and ordination. Then, priestly life, parish work, academic endeavors, and many, many talks, conversations, homilies, classes, occupations, and projects. I gained more knowledge, to be sure, but also experienced some sorrows and frustrations. There were many joys and accomplishments, but also many moments of confusion.

I have never doubted my faith, but it does not always feel as simple and evident as it did years ago. Faith is a challenge and, when faced with difficulties, is not always easy. And yet, it is there. How to believe more? How to never lose the strength of faith?

As a parish priest, I have seen this same process in many parishioners: time passes, their lives are filled with complications, busyness, and the monotony of routine. They read and hear of the scandals in the Church. They ask themselves, "Do I still believe?

If my faith does not seem as evident as before, does that mean that I have doubts? Where can I encounter the living Christ at times when the Church does not seem to show the radiance of His holiness? How can I believe more?"

The question about believing becomes acutely urgent in times of crisis. The doctrinal confusion and scandals rocking the barque of the Church create a situation in which faith appears particularly difficult and fragile. Though no longer exercising the authority of the Petrine office, Pope Emeritus Benedict XVI, as a Christian and a Bishop, has offered some penetrating reflections on the recent sexual scandals that have caused so much pain and confusion. Recognizing that "such misconduct by clerics ultimately damages the Faith," Benedict also indicated that the ultimate cause of the scandals is the lack of faith. Wondering how such horrific actions have been possible, and how the scandals could have reached such dramatic proportions, he simply said, "Only where faith no longer determines the actions of man are such offenses possible. . . . [U]ltimately, the reason is the absence of God."[1] Significantly, these reflections received great condemnation by several critics, who in the end, only proved his point. The long essays in opposition to Benedict's diagnosis, while trying to dissect the problem and offer other causes for the crisis,

---

[1] "Full text of Benedict XVI essay: 'The Church and the scandal of sexual abuse,'" *Catholic News Agency*, April 10, 2019, https://www.catholicnewsagency.com/news/full-text-of-benedict-xvi-the-church-and-the-scandal-of-sexual-abuse-59639.

only revealed the main problem: the absence of God. Indeed, as Benedict himself responded, the name of God and the words of Scripture were simply absent in the theological writings of his critics.[2] When God is not present, when faith is not a reality that determines daily life, then we cannot live according to the Gospel. And when God is not present in our analyses of reality, when faith is but another idea or area of knowledge, then we cannot understand what is happening, and even less can we find solutions for our problems.

Because of this, the first task for the Church today is, truly, the effort of purifying and renewing the faith. Only by going to the foundation of our Christian existence will we be able to find new horizons and answers for our difficult times—new answers, new hope, and new charity. Indeed, "the primary, the fundamental *ablatio* [removal] that is needed for the Church is the act of faith itself."[3]

I am convinced that understanding more deeply the richness of the *act of believing* can help renew our faith. I hope this little book, which does nothing more than present some of the insights on faith of a great believer and thinker—Joseph Ratzinger—can make a

---

[2] Anian Christoph Wimmer, "Benedict XVI responds to criticism of his essay on the Church and the sexual abuse crisis," *Catholic News Agency*, August 27, 2019, https://www.catholicnewsagency.com/news/benedict-responds-to-criticism-of-his-essay-on-the-church-and-the-sexual-abuse-crisis-51446.

[3] Joseph Ratzinger, *Called to Communion: Understanding the Church Today*, trans. Adrian Walker (San Francisco: Ignatius Press, 1991), 144.

small contribution to all those who, because they believe, would like to trust more in the loving presence of Jesus Christ and in what He has revealed to us.

METHODOLOGY

This brief volume surveys Ratzinger's own explorations of faith as an act. Therefore, I will not reflect on the contents of our faith, but rather on the act of believing: What does it mean to believe? How does faith begin? How does a Christian believe? These are some of the questions we should be able to answer.

The beginning of our exploration is a decisive book: *Introduction to Christianity*. I will say more about this work later. For now we should know that our quest will start with that book, and from there we will go on to Ratzinger's other writings. We will do so trying to keep the spirit of exploration, searching with the author for important keys to the problem of believing today. This book does not pretend to be a definitive and exhaustive treatise on faith, not even on faith according to Ratzinger. For he is not the kind of systematic thinker who tried to say everything in the manner of a scholastic treatise. Ratzinger, like his great master St. Augustine, is a man with questions, a man who has tried to respond to those queries in his different writings. He never intended to provide a final, systematic scheme with no further questions about a given topic.

What I have tried to do is simply to read Ratzinger's insights on faith, beginning with *Introduction to Christianity* and then going freely to his other writings, in order to offer some provisional but meaningful organization to his ideas, hoping thus to facilitate a better appreciation of his significant contribution. The first chapter of this book will describe the landscape in which we are called to believe today, with both its perennial and its specifically current challenges. The second chapter is a brief consideration of faith as a gift, both as given and received. The final chapter is a reflection on the act of believing, seen as an act that is personal, integral, and ecclesial.

Because this is a book on the idea of believing in the thought of Joseph Ratzinger, I have not used any of his magisterial teachings for the body of this work. I have also intentionally limited my recourse to secondary sources.[4] Finally, I have purposely tried to

---

[4] Among the growing bibliography on Joseph Ratzinger, see the following. For his life: Elio Guerriero, *Benedict XVI: His Life and Thought*, trans. William J. Melcher (San Francisco: Ignatius Press, 2018); Peter Seewald, *Benedict XVI: An Intimate Portrait*, trans. Henry Taylor and Anne Englund Nash (San Francisco: Ignatius Press, 2008); Pablo Blanco Sarto, *Joseph Ratzinger: Una Biografía* (Pamplona: Eunsa, 2004). For his thought: Aidan Nichols, *The Thought of Benedict XVI: An Introduction to the Theology of Joseph Ratzinger* (London: Burns & Oates, 2005); Tracey Rowland, *Ratzinger's Faith: The Theology of Pope Benedict XVI* (Oxford: Oxford University Press, 2008); Emery de Gaál, *The Theology of Pope Benedict XVI: The Christocentric Shift* (New York: Palgrave Macmillan, 2010); Vincent Twomey, *Benedict XVI: The Conscience of Our Age: A Theological Portrait* (San Francisco: Ignatius Press, 2007); Pablo Blanco Sarto, *Joseph Ratzinger: Razón y cristianismo: La Victoria de la inteligencia en el mundo de las religiones* [Reason and Christianity: The victory of the intelligence in the world of

write a short volume, one that will bring Ratzinger's reflections on faith to the forefront, and hopefully motivate greater interest in reading his works directly. What I expect is to present in a meaningful and logical way some of the most relevant and fascinating explorations on the act of believing that Joseph Ratzinger has offered the world and the Church, from his own faith, prayer, and study.

INTRODUCTION TO CHRISTIANITY: A MODEL FOR THEOLOGY

As already noted, this book is a study that begins with *Introduction to Christianity* and, from that foundational volume, goes on to explore further reflections on faith in Ratzinger's other works.

The most obvious reason for using this work as our starting point is that this modern classic, published fifty years ago, contains in seed some of the most fascinating contributions that will unfold through the following decades.[5] There is, however, another reason for this choice: *Introduction to Christianity* is an appealing model for theological work to-

---

religions] (Madrid: Rialp, 2005).

[5] First published as *Einführung in das Christentum* (Munich: Kösel-Verlag, 1968) and soon followed by an English translation, *Introduction to Christianity* (London: Burns & Oates, 1969). A new German edition was published in 2000; revisions to the English edition were published in 1990 and 2004 by Ignatius Press. All citations herein are to the 2004 English edition.

day. I will explain this by taking a little detour.

It is common to experience a real appreciation for the writings of the Fathers of the Church, those saints and first explorers of theology in the early Church. Although at times their style might feel quite different from what we are used to reading, there is a genuine fascination that comes from those voices of old. Whether we read letters from a bishop on his way to martyrdom, instructions on how to organize nascent Christian communities, stories of persecution, stories of conversion, explorations of dogma, or explanations of the sacramental mysteries, there is something compelling about these ancient witnesses.

Of course, we need to avoid a simplistic and romantic view of "the Fathers," as though they all wrote at the same place, in the same language, facing the same challenges, and with the same quality. Nevertheless, there is a freshness, a certain authenticity, and a personal and pastoral character that is, truly, "Patristic."

One explanation for this unique "flavor" of Patristic literature is its oral character. The vast majority of the ancient texts that we *read* today were *spoken* yesterday: two thirds of Patristic works were initially spoken, and even what was originally meant to become a "book" was dictated to someone. As Carol Harrison has put it, to read a Patristic text is, in a real sense, "eavesdropping on a conversation."[6]

These beautiful and ancient conversations in which we can participate as we read the Fathers re-

---

[6] Carol Harrison, *The Art of Listening in the Early Church* (Oxford: Oxford University Press, 2013), 2.

mind us of yet another important element. The works of the Fathers were not just curious exchanges among academics. They were almost always conversations between pastors and their people. In other words, the first concern of the Fathers was to illuminate the lives of their people, to help them know, love, and follow Christ in the Church, and to offer real responses to real challenges. That being said, this pastoral intention was not an obstacle to producing some of the most penetrating theological explorations ever made, since these works brought serious reflection on the faith to bear on the experiences of real life. These were not merely pragmatic, expedient solutions; they were rooted in the vision of the Gospel. Such is the beauty of oral theology.

We certainly need not limit living theology to what is ancient or to what was first spoken publicly. But we can agree that, generally speaking, this living, personal, and dialogical character gives a special quality to Patristic literature.

The influence and success of Joseph Ratzinger's *Introduction to Christianity* come, I suggest, from this same character: it was first given before people wrestling with significant questions and challenges. The popular professor of Tübingen knew that he had before him a great test and a fascinating opportunity: to explain the Catholic faith in a comprehensive and compelling way to university students of all fields of study. This long-awaited project was fulfilled in the summer of 1967.

Introduction to Christianity is indeed a very fine piece of theology, well researched and keenly explained. But its essence and genius is oral, and this,

I believe, makes it particularly compelling. In fact, the book is a transcription of the recordings of those lectures. In its first year, the book was reprinted a dozen times, and it has since been translated into approximately twenty languages.[7] It is an unusually successful work of theology; it is a real dialogue about the faith.

Reading *Introduction to Christianity* is not only an occasion to learn theology, but also an invitation to learn how to do theology. It offers a model for a thorough reflection on the deposit of faith, faithful to Tradition and yet distinctively new. It is an attempt to explore God's revelation in order to show its value and beauty to a world that has lost its familiarity with the faith; a vulnerable exercise of questioning and answering, of searching and finding, of confronting honest challenges, and discovering anew the strength of believing.

For these reasons, before explaining the content of what Christians believe, Ratzinger embarks on a reflection on what it means to believe. Anyone who searches for the truth ought to ask this question about believing—or not believing. This little book will attempt to offer, beginning with *Introduction to Christianity*, what Joseph Ratzinger has to say about the problem of believing today.

---

[7] See Guerriero, *Benedict XVI: His Life and Thought*, 198.

I. Believing in the Context of the Contemporary World

Among the vast wealth of themes that Joseph Ratzinger has developed during his lifetime, fundamental theology—the theological discipline that studies God's revelation and the rational foundations of the faith—holds a central place. He explains the reason why in his prologue to the first volume of his *Collected Works*: "I chose fundamental theology as my field because I wanted first and foremost to examine thoroughly the question: Why do we believe?"[1] The theme of faith—the object of this book—is a matter of significant importance in Ratzinger's thought, given that it is the core of the subject that he himself chose as the center of his theological research. With this in mind, let us

---

[1] Joseph Ratzinger, *Collected Works: Theology of the Liturgy*, ed. Michael J. Miller (San Francisco: Ignatius Press, 2014), xvi.

approach his classic *Introduction to Christianity* and from there, review his other works in order to deepen our understanding of what it means to believe.

1. DOUBT AND FAITH: THE PERENNIAL CHALLENGE OF BELIEVING

In his attempt to explain faith in a way accessible to the contemporary world, Joseph Ratzinger begins his *Introduction to Christianity* with a section on "Belief in the World of Today."[2] It is an attempt to situate the challenge of belief as the necessary foundation for his commentary on the contents of the Creed, which constitutes the main part of the book. The fact that Ratzinger's commentary on the Creed is preceded by an analysis of the contemporary experience of faith allows us to see his overarching intention: "[T]o help understand faith afresh as something that makes possible true humanity in the world of today, to expound faith without changing it into the small coin of empty talk painfully laboring to hide a complete spiritual vacuum."[3] In effect, an explanation of the faith

---

[2] Needless to say, much has changed in the world in the past fifty years. While in some ways the dramatic changes of the past decades suggest a prudent reception of Ratzinger's initial insights, it is also true that, essentially, his views on faith, modernity, and the human search for—and acceptance of—God have not only not lost their validity but can be perceived today even more in all their prophetic strength.

[3] Joseph Ratzinger, *Introduction to Christianity*, trans. J. R.

that did not take into account the context in which it is offered for belief would be of little help, perhaps reinforcing the commonplace prejudice that sees in faith nothing more than a number of irrelevant and outdated ideas and practices. The subsequent explication of the contents of the Symbol of Faith— i.e., the Creed—takes on a more meaningful and relevant character after reflection on the challenges that the act of faith has always presented, as well as a focused discussion of the particular challenges it faces today.

The challenges of faith are certainly not unique to this day and age, but the difficulties of our time seem to increase the constant vulnerability of faith and the uncertainty that always accompanies the believer—that insecurity that "in moments of temptation can suddenly and unexpectedly cast a piercing light on the fragility of the whole that usually seems so self-evident to him."[4]

Ratzinger illustrates this idea with two examples. The first is represented in a unique way in the faith of St. Thérèse of Lisieux. The saint who seemed to have always believed with such great ease, for whom faith appeared to be simple, naïve, and without any major difficulties, truly experienced the drama of having to trust amid insecurity, of having to see in darkness. Through this experience, her trust prevailed against temptations of unbelief; or better yet, she had to trust *precisely* because she was tempted, because she did not see, because what she had to accept was not always evident. Insecurity is not

---

Foster (San Francisco: Ignatius Press, 2004), 32.

[4] Ratzinger, *Introduction to Christianity*, 42.

only an occasional, destructive threat, but something that qualifies the authenticity of faith: one believes *because* one trusts when one doesn't see. In reality, "the believer can perfect his faith only on the ocean of nihilism, temptation, and doubt,[5] if he has been assigned the ocean of uncertainty as the only possible site for his faith."[6] This is expressed symbolically in a second example, that of the shipwrecked Jesuit missionary in Paul Claudel's play, *The Satin Slipper*. At the point of death, the missionary gives thanks to God for being tied to a cross and floating on the sea. "Fastened to the cross—with the cross fastened to nothing, drifting over the abyss. The situation of the contemporary believer could hardly be more accurately and impressively described."[7]

This insecurity is experienced not only by believers. Unbelievers see their unbelief in some ways "threatened" by the impossibility of ridding themselves of the suspicion that what the believer affirms might indeed be true: "[T]here is no escape from the dilemma of being a man. Anyone who makes up his mind to evade the uncertainty of belief will have to experience the uncertainty of unbelief, which can never finally eliminate for certain the possibility that belief may after all be the truth. It is not until belief is rejected that its unrejectability becomes evident."[8]

---

[5] The term "doubt" is a translation of the German *Zweifel*. Other accepted translations of *Zweifel* include "uncertainty," "distrust," "insecurity." See Joseph Ratzinger, *Einführung in das Christentum*, 17.

[6] Ratzinger, *Introduction to Christianity*, 44–45.

[7] Ratzinger, *Introduction to Christianity*, 43.

[8] Ratzinger, *Introduction to Christianity*, 45.

The unbeliever cannot definitively remove the problem of belief: "[E]ven in an unbelieving person there remains somehow a vestigial question of whether there is after all something there. Without taking this inner sensitivity into account we just cannot understand the history of mankind."[9] The problem of faith cannot be avoided, not only as an initial decision, but also as a constant dynamic of believing threatened by uncertainty, or not believing, with the risk of the possibility that faith is true. No one "can quite escape either doubt or belief; for the one, faith is present *against* doubt; for the other, *through* doubt and in the *form* of doubt."[10]

To believe is not an easy thing. In an interview with Peter Seewald, Ratzinger tells of an experience that a pastor had with the great theologian from Munich, Romano Guardini (1885–1968), who confided that when one grows older faith does not become easier, but rather more difficult.[11] The constant tension between faith and insecurity is part of the believer's path that does not necessarily fade over time, and in certain moments appears with greater intensity: "It is the basic pattern of man's destiny only to be allowed to find the finality of his existence in this unceasing rivalry between doubt and belief, temptation and certainty."[12]

The uncertainty inherent to the dilemma of faith is more than just a negative characteristic that we

---

[9] Joseph Ratzinger, *God and the World: A Conversation with Peter Seewald*, trans. Henry Taylor (San Francisco: Ignatius Press, 2002), 32.

[10] Ratzinger, *Introduction to Christianity*, 47.

[11] Ratzinger, *God and the World*, 37.

[12] Ratzinger, *Introduction to Christianity*, 47.

must accept. We believe *because* we trust, not because it all seems evident and easy to embrace. This dimension of faith establishes a valuable bridge that can help bring together believers and unbelievers: "Perhaps in precisely this way doubt, which saves both sides from being shut up in their own worlds, could become the avenue of communication."[13] We are brought into solidarity with unbelievers by the threat of insecurity, the persecution of unbelief, the need to believe when it is difficult,[14] and a confidence that at times feels distant;

---

[13] Ratzinger, *Introduction to Christianity*, 47.

[14] St. John Henry Newman, in his *Apologia pro Vita Sua*, describes his own experience of conversion, faith, and insecurity: "Ten thousand difficulties do not make one single doubt." When he refers to difficulty, he seems to allude to what Ratzinger calls *Zweifel*, often translated as "doubt," but which could be better understood as "insecurity." It is worth reading the complete testimony: "I was not conscious to myself, on my conversion, of any change, intellectual or moral, wrought in my mind. I was not conscious of firmer faith in the fundamental truths of Revelation, or of more self-command; I had not more fervor; but it was like coming into port after a rough sea; and my happiness on that score remains to this day without interruption. . . . Nor had I any trouble about receiving those additional articles, which are not found in the Anglican Creed. Some of them I believed already, but not any one of them was a trial to me. I made a profession of them upon my reception with the greatest ease, and I have the same ease in believing them now. I am far of course from denying that every article of the Christian Creed, whether as held by Catholics or by Protestants, is beset with intellectual difficulties; and it is simple fact, that, for myself, I cannot answer those difficulties. Many persons are very sensitive of the difficulties of Religion; I am as sensitive of them as any one; but I have never been able to see a connection between apprehending

these challenges form part of the nature of the act of faith and help us not to take it for granted:

> Faith is always a path. As long as we live we are on the way, and on that account faith is always under pressure and under threat. And it is healthy that it can never turn into a convenient ideology. That it does not make me hardened and unable to follow the thoughts of my doubting brother and to sympathize with him. Faith can only mature by suffering anew, at every stage in life, the oppression and the power of unbelief, by admitting its reality and then finally going right through it, so that it again finds the path opening ahead for a while.[15]

2. THE CONTEMPORARY FORM OF THE CRISIS OF FAITH

The tension between uncertainty and belief is integral to the very nature of believing. Particular characteristics of the present age, however, cause this uncertainty

---

those difficulties, however keenly, and multiplying them to any extent, and on the other hand doubting the doctrines to which they are attached. Ten thousand difficulties do not make one doubt, as I understand the subject; difficulty and doubt are incommensurate." John Henry Newman, *Apologia pro Vita Sua: Being a History of His Religious Opinions* (London: Longmans, Green, Reader, and Dyer, 1875), 214–215.

[15] Ratzinger, *God and the World*, 26.

to be experienced more acutely, and often doubt or denial are seen as adequate mental attitudes that marginalize faith from daily life. This situation is rooted in the limitation of our understanding of faith as it pertains to modernity and is manifested principally as agnosticism and relativism. In this context, the difficulty in believing and speaking about the faith grows, while the abyss over which faith must pass also seems to widen.

Description of the Situation

Undoubtedly, to speak of faith is something more and more foreign to ordinary people; it would seem that it has lost its pertinence and importance. At best, it is limited to being a theme that might be interesting to bring up every now and then; at worst, one that people try to avoid at all costs.

Introduction to Christianity opens with an analysis of this difficulty: "Anyone who tries today to talk about the question of Christian faith in the presence of people who are not thoroughly at home with ecclesiastical language and thought (whether by vocation or convention) soon comes to sense the alien—and alienating—nature of such an enterprise."[16] Ratzinger uses the "disturbing analogy" of a clown who, on seeing his circus in flames, is sent to a nearby village to ask for help and to alert the people to the danger of the fire. The village residents, however, think it is a trick to call their attention to the circus, and they

---

[16] Ratzinger, *Introduction to Christianity*, 39

clap and laugh while the clown desperately tries to convey that what he says is important, that the situation is urgent. As the laughter increases, the flames finally arrive at the village and consume it along with the circus.[17]

Ratzinger sees in the clown's failure to effectively communicate his message an image of what is frequently encountered by modern theologians who do not know how to make their speech relevant.[18] The solution for contemporary theology, however, does not consist in mere *aggiornamento* (bringing up to date), which sometimes is not much more than a cheap window-dressing of profane and secular language.[19] The problem is not only about form or an exterior crisis, and the solution is not just about appearing modern and using the buzz words of the latest ideological fashion. It is not only difficulties of language or translation that increase this vulnerability, but also other distortions characteristic of our times.

One of the greatest problems that we face today is that "faith has been left in the lurch by philosophy and suddenly finds itself, so to speak, in a vacuum."[20] Without the support of a worldview that acknowledg-

---

[17] Ratzinger, *Introduction to Christianity*, 39–40. The story cited is taken from Harvey Cox, who in turn took it from Kierkegaard.

[18] Regarding the challenge for modern theologians to explain the faith in a simple way, see Joseph Ratzinger, *What It Means to Be a Christian: Three Sermons*, trans. Henry Taylor (San Francisco: Ignatius Press, 2006), 66–71.

[19] See *Introduction to Christianity*, 41.

[20] Ratzinger, *Faith and the Future* (San Francisco: Ignatius Press, 2009), 61.

es that reality has a foundation that can be known, and that it is possible to grasp the essence of things, faith loses its place and becomes irrelevant. What is the point of believing if faith has no real foundation? Does it not then become an inconvenience, an arbitrary source of disagreements? From this is born the search for a certain "peace" in which faith no longer pretends to affirm anything definitive, and instead limits itself to the camp of sentimentality. However, "this is not a peace but rather a division of man in which reason and feeling suffer equal damage,"[21] and the faith ends up encased in "caricatures and perversions"[22] that in no way respond to the nature of man.

With that absence of a foundation, belief often passes on to be no more than a synonym for opinion, such as believing that the weather will be fine tomorrow: "Many people probably think that this meaning of 'believing' is also applicable in the realm of religion, so that the contents of the Christian faith are an imperfect, preliminary stage of knowledge."[23] Based on this informal conception of belief as opinion, we see the growth of "a widespread notion that the Christian faith is also a collection of conjectures about things that are not accessible as an exact science."[24] In that way, faith is presented

---

[21] Ratzinger, *A Turning Point for Europe? The Church in the Modern World: Assessment and Forecast*, trans. Brian McNeil, CRV (San Francisco: Ignatius Press, 2010), 113.

[22] Ratzinger, *A Turning Point for Europe?*, 109.

[23] Joseph Ratzinger, *Pilgrim Fellowship of Faith: The Church as Communion*, trans. Henry Taylor (San Francisco: Ignatius Press, 2005), 18.

[24] Joseph Ratzinger et al., *Handing on the Faith in an Age of*

as something that must be surpassed: "[F]aith seems to us something temporary and provisional that one ought really to be able to get beyond, even if frequently it is unavoidable precisely as a provisional attitude."[25] The evident "dissatisfaction with faith"[26] that we experience carries an urgent question: "Is faith an attitude worthy of a modern and mature human being?"[27]

The Limits of the Modern Understanding of Faith

In considering the question of the validity of faith for modern man, we need to understand modernity's approach to faith in the context of modernity's broader approach to reality.[28] For modernity, faith is considered a type of knowledge that fails to meet the fundamental criterion that validates all knowing: that which we can perceive with our senses. But to arrive at this point, Ratzinger explains, modernity has gone through two profound spiritual and cultural stages.

He describes the first step as the birth of histor-

Disbelief, trans. Michael J. Miller (San Francisco: Ignatius Press, 2006), 25.

[25] Joseph Ratzinger, *To Look on Christ: Exercises in Faith, Hope, and Love*, trans. Robert Nowell (New York: Crossroad, 1991), 11

[26] Ratzinger, *Faith and the Future*, 26.

[27] Ratzinger, *To Look on Christ*, 11.

[28] Modernity, broadly speaking, is the period—with its attitudes and practices—that began toward the end of the seventeenth century and was influenced by the Enlightenment.

icism. This moment was prepared by Descartes and reached its fullest expression in Kant, but Ratzinger draws particular attention to the role of Giambattista Vico (1668–1744). Vico denotes, according to Ratzinger, "the real end of the old metaphysics and the beginning of the specifically modern attitude of mind."[29] This first step consists in leaving the ancient idea of truth, *verum est ens* (being is truth), to pass on to *verum quia factum* (truth is what has been made). In other words, we can only truly know that which we have made. Vico formally bases this proposition on Aristotle: from the need for knowledge of causes, he concludes that we can only know something if we know the cause of it.[30] Therefore, "the old equation of truth and being is replaced by the new one of truth and factuality."[31] With it comes the dominance of fact, and thus history, alongside mathematics, acquired a scientific weight that it had never had before.

The second step consists in the move toward technical thinking, expressed as moving from *verum quia factum* to *verum quia faciendum* (truth is what is being made).[32] What matters here is not what man has made, but what can be made, the makable over the made. Therefore, it is the future, not the past, which is now seen as definitive. Here, the influence of Karl Marx (1818–1883) is critical. In this step, the *techne* supplants history; truth is what is repeatable, and thus the only decisive and sure criterion for knowledge is

---

[29] Ratzinger, *Introduction to Christianity*, 55.
[30] See Ratzinger, *Introduction to Christianity*, 61.
[31] Ratzinger, *Introduction to Christianity*, 61.
[32] Ratzinger, *Introduction to Christianity*, 65–66.

the natural scientific method. From this perspective, knowing what can be made, knowing the new man that can be created, is more important than knowing the historical origins.

From here we can see where the process has gone: "[T]he reduction of man to a 'fact' is the precondition for understanding him as a *faciendum* (as something "makable") that is to be led out of its own resources into a new future."[33] These two stages culminate in what Ratzinger calls an essential "characteristic of our contemporary scientific attitude . . . the limitation to 'phenomena,' to what is evident and can be grasped."[34] It is a conception of reality made by the generalization of the scientific method as the definitive criterion for knowledge, suggesting that we can only truly know that which can be repeated. Consequently, "the scientific method, which consists of a combination of mathematics (Descartes!) and devotion to the facts in the form of the repeatable experiment, appears to be the one real vehicle of reliable certainty."[35] It is here that the scientific method becomes absolute, bringing with it "a self-limitation of positive reason, which is adequate in the technical domain, but which, when it gets generalized, mutilates man."[36]

This conception of reality that is born from limiting truth to phenomena, what we can sense and that which can be proven, implies "a new concept of truth

---

[33] Ratzinger, *Introduction to Christianity*, 66

[34] Ratzinger, *Introduction to Christianity*, 58.

[35] Ratzinger, *Introduction to Christianity*, 64.

[36] Joseph Ratzinger, "Europe in the Crisis of Cultures," *Communio* 32 (Summer 2005): 351, https://www.theway.org.uk/endeanweb/ratzinger32-2.pdf.

and reality" in which we cease "seeking the hidden 'in-itselfness' of things and sounding the nature of being itself; such activities seem to us to be a fruitless enterprise."[37] We now arrive at a point where we "no longer seek truth but only inquire about the correctness of the methods applied . . . The renunciation of truth itself and a reliance upon what is verifiable and upon the correctness of methods are typical of the modern natural scientific outlook."[38] The "methodic self-limitation"[39] of modern thought results in brushing aside the great questions of humanity, giving up any hope of an answer, and concentrating exclusively on that which we can prove through natural science. The influence of this conception of reality limited to phenomena is so significant that the "scientific rationality" of modernity has generated a "technological culture made possible by science [that] places its stamp on what is now truly the whole world."[40]

Agnosticism

A logical consequence of making the scientific method the only path for true knowledge is the abandonment of transcendence or the limitation of its pursuit to the demands of the scientific method. Without necessarily denying God in an explicit way, faith is demoted to the level of opinion and thus cast to the

---

[37] Ratzinger, *Introduction to Christianity*, 58.
[38] Ratzinger, *Faith and the Future*, 27.
[39] Ratzinger, *A Turning Point for Europe?*, 115.
[40] Ratzinger, "Europe in the Crisis of Cultures," 347.

side. In his last conference before being elected pope, Ratzinger described this technical culture, which was born in Europe, but then spread to the whole world:

> And, in the wake of this form of rationality, Europe has developed a culture that, in a way hitherto unknown to humanity, excludes God from public consciousness, whether he is totally denied or whether his existence is judged to be indemonstrable, uncertain, and so is relegated to the domain of subjective choices, as something in any case irrelevant for public life. This purely functional rationality, to give it a name, has revolutionized moral conscience in a way that is equally new with respect to all hitherto existing cultures, inasmuch as it claims that only what is experimentally provable is rational.[41]

The logic of this functional rationality marginalizes the problem of faith. Atheism, as the total denial of God, is not that common in our time;[42]

---

[41] Ratzinger, "Europe in the Crisis of Cultures," 347.

[42] Exponents of a "new atheism" enjoyed a surge of popularity around the turn of the millennium. Authors such as Richard Dawkins, Christopher Hitchens, Victor Stenger, and others, militantly and with great influence promoted an aggressive campaign against religion. For critical insights regarding these ideas see Thomas Crean, *God Is No Delusion: A Refutation of Richard Dawkins* (San Francisco: Ignatius, 2007) and David Bentley Hart, *Atheist Delusions: The Christian Revolution and Its Fashionable Enemies* (New Haven: Yale University Press, 2009).

agnosticism, on the other hand, presents itself as something rational and sincere. "The honesty of ratiocination and humility in the face of the unknown seem to recommend agnosticism, while explicit atheism already knows too much and clearly contains a dogmatic element within itself."[43] In view of this, it would seem practical to think that the only answer to the problem of God and faith is to realize that we cannot really know anything for certain and therefore, it would be "more fitting for the mature man or woman of our age to refrain from a judgment on matters of this kind and to await the moment when science will hold in its hand definite answers even to this range of questions."[44] This conception differs from the certain and sometimes aggressive attitude of scientific atheism; it believes instead that one must serenely accept that, in reality, faith exceeds that which honestly—through the scientific method—can be known. Therefore, the right thing to do would be to leave it off to the side and live from what we actually can know. Accordingly, agnosticism seems to be the only just attitude for those who are honest and even pious.[45] It would not be necessary to consciously deny God, but simply to leave Him as a God with nothing to do.[46]

However appealing these ideas may appear, a more attentive analysis shows that agnosticism, though it can be attractive as a theory, is impossible

---

[43] Ratzinger, *To Look on Christ*, 15.
[44] Ratzinger, *To Look on Christ*, 15.
[45] See Ratzinger, *To Look on Christ*, 16.
[46] See Ratzinger, *Introduction to Christianity*, 16.

in practice.[47] Ratzinger approaches his criticism of agnosticism from a very existential perspective. When considering the apparent honesty of the modern renunciation of the inscrutable and transcendent, one must object, firstly, that "the thirst for the infinite belongs quite simply to essential human nature."[48] The question about what goes beyond the demonstrable—about the possibility of the infinite—cannot simply be silenced. In effect, "[C]an we simply live hypothetically 'as if there were no God' even if perhaps there is?"[49] Honesty of thought ought to lead to the asking of fundamental questions about life, without science overstepping its proper limits and silencing the inquiry.

This question of the infinite and the desire to expound upon it further is reinforced by the consideration of its practical nature. A question about faith and God is not a mere theoretical issue, but rather an eminently practical one, with consequences for the actual life of each person. Everything in the concrete existence of an individual or in a culture depends on the answer to the question of God. Agnosticism, however, attempts to avoid answering it. But Ratzinger notes that this position is incoherent, since even if "I allow agnosticism to be valid in theory, in practice I must nevertheless decide between two possibilities: to live as if there were no God or to live as if God did exist and was the determining reality for

---

[47] See Ratzinger, *To Look on Christ*, 16.

[48] Ratzinger, *To Look on Christ*, 16.

[49] Ratzinger, *To Look on Christ*, 17

my life."[50] There is no other possibility than living as though God exists or as though God does not exist. Agnosticism, even though tempting because of its apparent lack of commitment, is not a real solution to the problem of God.[51] In God's presence one must say "yes" or "no" and accept the practical consequences of his choice: "We are not allowed neutrality when faced with the question of God."[52]

Relativism

The absolutizing of the scientific method, with its consequent renunciation or reformulation of the question of ultimate truth, bears another consequence: relativism. As any reader familiar with Ratzinger is aware, this is a theme he frequently addressed.

In the preface to the new edition of *Introduction to Christianity* published in 2000, having noted the time that had lapsed since the first edition of his work, Ratzinger marked the importance of the years 1968 and 1989 as landmarks that summarize the recent history of humanity. The dream of freedom and

---

[50] Ratzinger, *To Look on Christ*, 17.
[51] See Joseph Murphy, *Christ Our Joy: The Theological Vision of Pope Benedict XVI* (San Francisco: Ignatius Press, 2008), 63.
[52] Ratzinger, *To Look on Christ*, 18. See Marcello Pera's opinion concerning Ratzinger's proposal to non-believers, to try to live *veluti si Deus daretur* (as if God existed). Marcello Pera, "Introduction," in Joseph Ratzinger, *Christianity and the Crisis of Cultures*, trans. Brian McNeil (San Francisco: Ignatius Press, 2006), 7–22.

a new justice that fueled the student revolution of 1968, and the collapse of the promises of socialist regimes in 1989, left behind a heritage of deception and uncertainty. No one believes in the great moral promises anymore, and most people prefer to seek justice and peace in the pragmatic, without asking about truth, adding to the confusion and skepticism around these great ideals.[53] Indeed, after witnessing the fall of what seemed so full of promise and hope, shouldn't we try to simply co-exist, being content with our own preferences, and merely tolerating other opinions? Wouldn't it be more effective to learn how to agree to disagree, renouncing the problematic burden of seeking for the truth? The failure of what seemed like the sole scientific base for the solution to the problems of humanity "could only favor nihilism or at any rate absolute relativism."[54]

At this crossroad, Ratzinger insistently maintains that "relativism has become the central problem for faith in our time."[55] Its centrality and powerful influence come from two characteristics: its persistent attitude, and its widespread diffusion. With respect to the former, a typical relativistic disposition denies the existence of an absolute truth without betraying any nostalgia for a metaphysical past: "It by no means appears simply as resignation in the face of the unfathomable nature of truth, of course; rather,

---

[53] See Ratzinger, *Introduction to Christianity*, 11–19.

[54] Joseph Ratzinger, *Truth and Tolerance: Christian Belief and World Religions*, trans. Henry Taylor (San Francisco: Ignatius Press, 2004), 117.

[55] Ratzinger, *Truth and Tolerance*, 117.

it defines itself positively on the basis of the concepts of tolerance, dialectic epistemology, and freedom, which would be limited by maintaining one truth as being valid for everyone."[56]

Along with the strong self-affirmation of contemporary relativism, we find its widespread diffusion. It is not only a theme for academics but has also become the common mentality of the modern person.

To be sure, a certain relativism has its proper place in the political and social spheres, inasmuch as there are a multitude of options to be considered for the betterment of society. But just as the scientific method has overstepped its limits, relativism today has likewise gone beyond its boundaries[57] and has become the only acceptable way of understanding reality. In short, it has become a type of new religion for modern man. No one can say that he knows the truth, because that would be a clear sign of fanaticism or fundamentalism, two of the greatest "sins" in a democratic and pluralistic society under the sway of this new religion of relativism.

This brings us to what Ratzinger, in his important homily at the beginning of the 2005 conclave, called the "dictatorship of relativism":

> Today, having a clear faith based on the Creed of the Church is often labeled as fundamentalism. Whereas relativism, that is, letting oneself be "tossed here and there, carried about by every wind of doctrine," seems

---

[56] Ratzinger, *Truth and Tolerance*, 117.
[57] See Ratzinger, *Truth and Tolerance*, 117.

the only attitude that can cope with modern times. We are building a dictatorship of relativism that does not recognize anything as definitive and whose ultimate goal consists solely of one's own ego and desires.[58]

Relativism intrinsically forbids the affirmation of the existence of truth and therefore prohibits the universal truth, cohesive and valid in history, realized in the person of Jesus Christ, and transmitted by the faith of the Church. The Christian faith is considered a type of fundamentalism that goes against the modern spirit and poses a threat to tolerance and liberty.

Relativism, like agnosticism, contradicts itself in practice; we see, on the one hand, the need (not at all relativistic!) to believe in the truth that "all truth is relative." Because of this inherent contradiction, relativism is an inadequate basis for living. It degenerates into dictatorship, an unquestionable dogmatism that silences the desire for something that transcends mere opinion and could offer a greater certainty for the actual fruits of our dialogues: "For where relativism is consistently thought through and lived (without clinging secretly to an ultimate trust that comes from faith), either it becomes nihilism or else it expands positivism into the power that dominates everything."[59] Indeed, what could remain if all was rel-

---

[58] Ratzinger, Homily at the Mass "Pro Eligendo Romano Pontifice," April 18, 2005 (available at http://www.vatican.va/gpII/documents/homily-pro-eligendo-pontifice_20050418_en.html).

[59] Ratzinger, *A Turning Point for Europe?*, 109.

ative, if in the absence of objective truth, then there was nothing that our own personal opinions could neither question nor define? We would have a totalitarianism of the majority, the uncertain situation in which "nothing is good or evil in itself,"[60] where everything depends on consequences or circumstances, on what each one perceives, or on what the majority decides. Relativism leads to a vacuum: if there is no truth, then there is no joy. How could we find true joy if the ground on which we stand is so uncertain; if the meaning of goodness depends on each one's choice; if we have to define ourselves and invent our happiness? The absence of truth is the greatest illness of our times.[61] Without truth, it is impossible to believe with certainty in anyone or anything. The common inability to trust and to have deep interpersonal relationships, the loneliness, and the abuses of basic rights in the name of tolerance are some of the characteristics of a society that believes that one cannot believe anymore.

---

[60] Ratzinger, "Europe in the Crisis of Cultures," 348.

[61] "Joseph Ratzinger has devoted himself to the question of truth, without which genuine joy is impossible. The real problem of mankind, he maintains, is the darkening of truth, indeed, lack of truth is the major disease of our age" (Murphy, *Christ Our Joy*, 44).

II. Faith as Gift Given and Gift Received

In the previous chapter we looked at the various challenges to faith, both the perennial challenges as well as those characteristic of the modern age. In particular, we saw that the rise of agnosticism and relativism generate a cultural environment in which believing becomes even more trying.

But faith, as challenging as it may appear, is still and will always be an invitation for everyone: a reality for many, a challenge for others. Ratzinger's insights into the act of believing as a gift given and received offer some pathways toward a renewed openness and appreciation of faith.

1. Faith as a Gift Given

To believe is an act through which we realize our deepest meaning. However, this *act* has the character of an *answer*: that is, it is a response to the initiative of God. Therefore, the first aspect of faith that we must consider is its inherent character as a free gift from God.

Faith is a gift that God gives to us. There are various ways that we can rationally explore the existence of God, but in order to actually believe in Him we need the free gift of faith. God's giving of the gift takes precedence over human initiative, though our reception of the gift is a necessary part of the process.[1]

As we saw earlier, agnosticism and relativism tend to silence any questioning that exceeds the limits of the scientific method or the supposed honesty of thought that accepts its own weakness. Notwithstanding, a restlessness remains, since it is evident that "the rationality of the world cannot be sensibly and usefully explained on the basis of irrationality."[2] The dilemma of faith cannot simply be rejected.

As we have seen, though, believing is not always easy. There is an inner openness of the soul to God: "[B]y natural reason man can know God with certainty, on the basis of his works" (CCC 50). But we also know that this knowledge is only a preamble to the act of faith. In effect, "unbelief is unnatural, but at the same it is always true that human beings cannot completely dispel the strange twilight that hangs over the question of the eternal, that God must cross over to them and talk to them if real relations are to

---

[1] Regarding this, see Pablo Blanco Sarto, "*Logos* and *Dia-Logos*: Faith, Reason, (and Love) According to Joseph Ratzinger," http://www.anglicantheologicalreview.org/static/pdf/articles/sarto.pdf.

[2] Ratzinger, *To Look on Christ*, 28.

be established with him."³ When God reaches out to us with the gift of faith, our God-given thirst for the infinite, and the knowledge of God that natural reason can attain, receive a new greatness and have access to the mysteries that only God can show, namely "another order of knowledge, which man cannot possibly arrive at by his own powers: the order of divine Revelation [Cf. *Dei Filius*: DS 3015]" (CCC 50).

We do not believe because it is easy or because our intelligence can fathom all the mysteries that reality presents: we believe because we have received a gift that is greater than anything we could possibly imagine, and because of it we are able to truly respond to the great challenges that are presented to us.

Therefore, the free gift of faith ought to be received with joy and humility. For this, Ratzinger recommends "openness to the infinite, vigilance, and sensitivity for the whole of being: a humility of thought that is ready to bow before the majesty of truth, before which we are not judges but suppliants."⁴ Following the Church Fathers, he proposes to us a meditation on the blessedness of "the pure of heart" (see Matt 5:8) in relationship to faith: "The 'pure' heart is the one that is open and humble";⁵ the heart that with simplicity is capable of embracing the gift of faith, and is able to actualize all of faith's depth in daily life. "The possibility of 'seeing' God, that is, of knowing him at all, depends on one's purity of heart, which means a comprehensive process

---

3. Ratzinger, *To Look on Christ*, 29.
4. Ratzinger, *To Look on Christ*, 23.
5. Ratzinger, *To Look on Christ*, 24.

in which man becomes transparent, in which he does not remain locked upon himself, in which he learns to give himself and, in doing so, becomes able to see."[6]

2. CHRISTIAN FAITH AS A GIFT RECEIVED

We are free to embrace or refuse this free gift of faith. If we decide to acknowledge faith to be the act that gives meaning to existence, we must configure our lives to what faith presents. That requires conversion, opening ourselves to the greater horizon that comes with this gift. This supernatural act of faith finds a solid base in a type of daily, "natural" faith.

Faith in Daily Life

One of the first aspects of the human act of believing is a kind of natural faith upon which our common existence is built. In daily life we believe many things that we cannot prove and that we do not know firsthand. Just think of the many technologies that we do not fully understand, or the electronic advances that have become indispensable to us and that we use despite not knowing how they work. We could also think of the student trusting his teacher

---

[6] Joseph Ratzinger, *Principles of Catholic Theology: Building Stones for a Fundamental Theology*, trans. Sister Mary Frances McCarthy, SND (San Francisco: Ignatius Press, 1987), 350.

and using the periodic table in performing chemical equations; or a general audience trusting that the details reported by the news anchor of events taking place in remote areas of the world are true. "We live in a network of things we do not know about but that we rely on because our experience of them is in general positive. We 'believe' that all this will be okay, and through this kind of 'faith' we are able to have a share and interest in the product of other people's knowledge."[7]

Confidence plays a decisive role in this daily, universal faith: "[H]uman life becomes impossible if one can no longer trust other people and is no longer able to rely on their experience, on their knowledge, on what is already provided for us."[8] Faith is absolutely essential. We do not always have to start at the beginning; rather, we can rely on what others have known before us. We accept implicitly that our own knowing is not infallible or absolute, that others can know more than we ourselves know, and that only the whole of what we know together enables true progress and wellbeing. In this same sense, this faith of daily life is also "the expression of a lack of knowledge"[9] that permits us to understand the need of believing and trusting.

This faith of daily life has a proper structure. First, there is always someone who knows and is therefore worthy of trust. Next comes the trust of many who on a daily basis act upon a knowledge that

---

[7] Ratzinger, *To Look on Christ*, 12.
[8] Ratzinger, *To Look on Christ*, 12.
[9] Ratzinger, *To Look on Christ*, 12.

they have not directly obtained. Third, a daily experience constantly verifies that knowledge.[10] For example, an architect designs a building, where contractors install an elevator. Without specific knowledge of its mechanics, we use the elevator every day. This daily practice confirms us in our trust in what was not done by us. This human kind of faith is a preamble for the act of Christian faith, which demands, however, a different and deeper manner of trusting.

Accepting Christian Faith as Conversion

Day-to-day faith is natural and easy to comprehend. Christian faith, however—though it is rooted in our human nature—requires from the believer a radical change, a deep conversion.

Supernatural faith is another "mode of access to reality" where we find "the decisive enlargement of [our] whole view of the world"[11]; one that is very different from the horizontal vision that seeks to explain everything in terms of what is measurable. What distinguishes believers is not just partial affirmations on diverse aspects of reality, or certain particular opinions, but "a fundamental mode of behavior toward being, toward existence, toward one's own sector of reality, and toward reality as a whole."[12] Faith as "an act that comprehends all the dimensions of our

---

[10] See Ratzinger, *To Look on Christ*, 14.
[11] Ratzinger, *Introduction to Christianity*, 50.
[12] Ratzinger, *Introduction to Christianity*, 50.

existence"[13] implies a break in which "the center of gravity of reality, indeed, the concept of reality itself, change[s]."[14] For this reason, "belief has always had something of an adventurous break or leap about it, because in every age it represents the risky enterprise of accepting what plainly cannot be seen as the truly real and fundamental."[15]

This brings us to what Ratzinger describes as the "scandals," that is, the obstacles or gulfs that the believer must cross in order to believe. The first challenge is to make the choice for "what is not seen" as the foundation of "what is seen": the invisible must become the basis of the visible. The materialistic viewpoint seeks to explain everything from what it sees, from what it can measure and prove scientifically. The believer seeks another path: "Belief signifies the decision that at the very core of human existence there is a point that cannot be nourished and supported on the visible and tangible, that encounters and comes into contact with what cannot be seen and finds that it is a necessity for its own existence."[16]

---

[13] Joseph Ratzinger, *Gospel, Catechesis, Catechism: Sidelights on the Catechism of the Catholic Church*, trans. Adrian Walker (San Francisco: Ignatius Press, 1997), 24.

[14] Ratzinger, *Faith and the Future*, 40.

[15] Ratzinger, *Introduction to Christianity*, 52.

[16] Ratzinger, *Introduction to Christianity*, 51. For this allowance of "that which cannot be seen" as foundation of "that which can be seen," Ratzinger has been accused of Platonism and idealism, and of being thus poorly oriented to the concrete and the critical. A summary of the criticisms of Walter Kasper can be found in Pablo Blanco Sarto, *Joseph Ratzinger: Razón y cristianismo*, 125.

This leap over the abyss between the visible and the invisible permits an openness to a greater meaning of life. "Today, too, faith signifies a breaking out of the visible and calculable into a wider sphere. Today, it still means breaking open the horizon and reaching out across all frontiers."[17] In effect, if our sense and explanation of reality are not limited to what is material, visible, or measurable, but rather are open to what we cannot see or measure, then life acquires a greater horizon that can respond to the thirst for the infinite that we carry within.

Indeed, to believe "signifies a breaking out of the calculable, everyday world to make contact with the Eternal."[18] Faith permits us to welcome God, whom we do not see (see 1 John 4:20), as the response to the question about the meaning of reality: "There is no answer to this that will resolve every contradiction into incontrovertible, unambivalent truth with scientific clarity. Assent to the hiddenness of God is an essential part of the movement of the spirit that we call 'faith.'"[19]

The second abyss is the one between the past and the present. Faith fundamentally refers to tradition, that is to say the past, what might seem expired or overcome. In past ages, the idea of tradition brought with it the security of trustworthiness and stability. In contrast, our times look at tradition with mistrust, as "what has been laid aside, the merely out-of-date, whereas progress is regarded as the real promise of

---

[17] Ratzinger, *Faith and the Future*, 53.
[18] Ratzinger, *Faith and the Future*, 42.
[19] Ratzinger, *What It Means to Be a Christian*, 47.

life."[20] This aspect of faith is "scandalous" to many who would find it impossible to trust in the past because progress would be the only thing that matters to them. Thus, "the primary stumbling block to belief, the distance between the visible and the invisible, between God and Not-God, is concealed and blocked by the secondary stumbling block of Then and Now, by the antithesis between tradition and progress, by the loyalty to yesterday that belief seems to include."[21]

It is important to note that, while it is true that the links with the past that faith presupposes are undeniable and foundational, our "faith is essentially related to the future . . . it is a promise."[22] Faith is anchored in the past, but it points to the future. Even more, faith "signifies the superordination of the future over the present."[23] To believe, therefore, is a leap over an abyss that implies living "in a spirit of trust" and "setting out upon a journey and going beyond that false sense of being settled which holds a man to what is 'small but my own,' thus depriving him of true greatness."[24] The greatness of a confident openness to the future brought by faith leads us to live life as a journey and to adopt the attitude of a pilgrim.[25]

This priority on the future rather than the present is anchored in the past. The leap does not imply a rupture, but rather continuity; we walk toward

---

[20] Ratzinger, *Introduction to Christianity*, 53.
[21] Ratzinger, *Introduction to Christianity*, 53–54.
[22] Ratzinger, *Faith and the Future*, 42.
[23] Ratzinger, *Faith and the Future*, 42.
[24] Ratzinger, *Faith and the Future*, 42.
[25] Ratzinger, *Faith and the Future*, 74.

the future knowing what God has done in our past. And that leads us to consider the true "scandal" of the faith, its main abyss: the indispensable positive, that is, concrete and tangible, character of Christianity. Ratzinger tells us that "Christian belief is not merely concerned, as one might at first suspect from all the talk of belief or faith, with the eternal, which as the 'entirely Other' would remain completely outside the human world and time; on the contrary, it is much more concerned with God in history, with God as man."[26] This is what is truly shocking, that everything depends on one singular man in history. The nearness of God who becomes man and encounters us poses a challenge: we are impelled to believe not only in a certain vague, spontaneous, personal spirituality, nor in a generic presence of the eternal (which would perhaps be easier!), but in the mystery of God's salvation coming to us in a concrete place and moment in history: God reduced to a point.[27] This is one of the most fundamental aspects of the Christian faith, the personal revelation of God in history: "By thus seeming to bridge the gulf between eternal and temporal, between visible and invisible, by making us meet God as a man, the eternal as the temporal, as one of us, it understands itself as revelation."[28]

These abysses that we must cross over show us that conversion is necessary for Christian faith, a deep change that overcomes our natural tendency to trust only what is visible and permits us to put faith

---

[26] Ratzinger, *Introduction to Christianity*, 54.
[27] See Ratzinger, *Introduction to Christianity*, 55.
[28] Ratzinger, *Introduction to Christianity*, 54.

in things we do not control, to bet on a concrete man in history in whom all meaning and hope are found. Conversion is indispensable for belief: "[W]ithout this change of direction, without this resistance to the natural inclination, there can be no belief."[29]

To believe means not only theoretically accepting certain doctrines; it involves a re-formation of our entire existence. Referring to the liturgical origin of the text of the Creed as a part of the rite of Baptism, Ratzinger notes that the triple renunciation (of Satan, of his works, of his empty promises) and the triple affirmation (of belief in the three Persons of the Trinity) help us understand that "faith is located in the act of conversion."[30] Conversion, "the first word in Christianity,"[31] is what the Bible calls *metánoia*, and "is not just any Christian attitude but the fundamental Christian act per se, understood admittedly from a very definite perspective: that of transformation, conversion, renewal and change. To be a Christian, one must change not in some particular area but without reservation even to the innermost depths of one being."[32]

The profound change entailed by faith brings us to a fundamental question: "Which direction of existence does a man choose who resolves to tune the instrument of his life to the keynote of faith?"[33] Conversion permits us to recognize that "the act of faith is an opening out into the distance, a breaking

---

[29] Ratzinger, *Introduction to Christianity*, 51.
[30] Ratzinger, *Introduction to Christianity*, 88.
[31] Ratzinger, *Al servicio del Evangelio* [At the service of the Gospel] (Lima: Vida y Espiritualidad, 2003) (my translation).
[32] Ratzinger, *Principles of Catholic Theology*, 60.
[33] Ratzinger, *Faith and the Future*, 35.

down of the door of my subjectivity."[34] In that way, with the barriers of our limited subjectivity broken, we can truly find ourselves centered on God. To believe, then, means "achieving [a] Copernican revolution and no longer seeing ourselves as the center of the universe, around which everyone else must turn, because instead of that we have begun to accept quite seriously that we are one of many among God's creatures, all of which turn around God as their center."[35]

Being open to the immensity that God gives to those who recognize Him as the true center, we are then introduced to the freedom of living not only for ourselves (see 2 Cor 5:15). We have the fundamental choice to go against our spontaneous inertia and trust instead in what is transcendent, which leads us to a new and fuller existence. This act leads to becoming a Christian, opening ourselves to the fullness of what it means to be truly human; this is why "faith is the fundamental act of Christian existence."[36] It makes sense, then, to hear again what the then-professor of Tübingen told his audience, and might not seem evident otherwise: that Christian existence is expressed with the word "credo" and that the nucleus of what is Christian is defined in what "faith" is.[37]

---

[34] Ratzinger, *To Look on Christ*, 37.
[35] Ratzinger, *What It Means to Be a Christian*, 71.
[36] Ratzinger, *To Look on Christ*, 10.
[37] Ratzinger, *Introduction to Christianity*, 49.

Faith as Standing Firm and Understanding

Conversion opens the door for believers to a new existence that permits us to welcome the gift of faith through a personal and free choice. This allows for a deeper understanding of the nature of Christian faith as action.

Ratzinger gives great importance to the idea that faith is not understood from the relationship between knowing and doing, between Vico's *verum quia factum* and Marx's *verum quia faciendum*. Faith is not simply something that one knows, as a dead event of history, nor is it something that one does, as a project for social progress. Putting faith into one of these boxes prevents us from entering into the mystery of what we mean when we say *credo*—I believe.

Ratzinger follows a specifically biblical approach in his exploration of faith by using two rich terms: "stand" and "understand,"[38] which are two general concepts and two possibilities for the human being, related and yet distinct.

Ratzinger finds the basis for understanding the faith as "standing firm" and "understanding" in an Old Testament text that is difficult to translate: "If you do not stand firm in faith, you shall not stand at all" (Isa 7:9, NRSVCE). The Hebrew root *'mn* (as in "amen") carries a rich set of meanings that, when intermingled, give the verse its grandeur. Ideas like truth, strength, firmness, and entrusting oneself in total abandonment to something other, allow us to

---

[38] Regarding this, see Aidan Nichols, *The Thought of Benedict XVI*, 108.

plumb the depths of what it means to believe. "Faith in God appears as a holding on to God through which man gains a firm foothold for his life. Faith is thereby defined as taking up a position, as taking a stand trustfully on the ground of the word of God."[39]

To believe is to trust in what does not proceed from what we know or do. Here it is important to clarify that "meaning is not derived from knowledge."[40] The meaning of life is not something that we can create with our knowledge or action. An attempt of that nature would be as absurd as the tale of Baron de Münchhausen who wanted to get out of the swamp by pulling on his hair: "Meaning that is self-made is in the last analysis no meaning. Meaning, that is, the ground on which our existence as a totality can stand and live, cannot be made but only received."[41] As human beings, we need meaning as our bread, in order to actually subsist. In this way, Ratzinger brings us to understanding faith as standing firm: faith is our sustenance, our bread, for it gives us meaning without which life is not worth living. Faith is our foundation because on it we base our very existence.

Therefore, to believe as a Christian is understood as trusting the meaning that sustains us, "taking it as the firm ground on which I can stand fearlessly"; or, to put it in more theological language, "to believe as a Christian means understanding our existence as a response to the word, the *logos*, that upholds and maintains all things."[42]

---

[39] Ratzinger, *Introduction to Christianity*, 69.
[40] Ratzinger, *Introduction to Christianity*, 73.
[41] Ratzinger, *Introduction to Christianity*, 73.
[42] Ratzinger, *Introduction to Christianity*, 73.

In addition to standing firm, faith is understanding. In the act of believing, we encounter the meaning to which we have been entrusted. When we speak of understanding, Ratzinger refers to the act of "grasp[ing] the ground on which we have taken our stand as meaning and truth; that we learn to perceive that *ground* represents *meaning*."[43]

Certainly, faith is about an understanding that contrasts with that of the secular society, which proposes an extension of the fundamental methodical attitude of the natural sciences to reality as a whole, demanding that we trust only what is factual. Faith constitutes a radical rupture with this approach to reality: "[I]t is undeniable that Christian belief is a double affront to the attitude that the present world situation seems to force us to adopt. . . . The primacy of the invisible over the visible and that of receiving over making run directly counter to this basic situation."[44] The choice of faith brings us to a place that cannot be apprehended except as an invitation to see what we would not be able to grasp on our own. To believe is to trust in something radically different from what we can see or do with our own strength.

However, believing does not mean surrendering to the irrational. Believing as a Christian leads us to understand that faith truly is the foundation of reality. It is not about a simplistic choice in the face of what surpasses our reason, leaving us to rely on "mystery" as a last recourse. It is about giving mystery its place in reality and in our understanding, since the

---

[43] Ratzinger, *Introduction to Christianity*, 77.
[44] Ratzinger, *Introduction to Christianity*, 74.

truth of mystery does not seek to destroy knowledge, but rather to facilitate faith as understanding.[45] If we open ourselves to mystery, then reason can arrive at what would otherwise be lost, limited by scientific knowledge. "The *mysterium*, as faith sees it, is not the irrational but rather the uttermost depths of the divine reason, which our weak eyes are no longer able to penetrate."[46] Faith does not contradict reason; rather, it presupposes it and takes it to an even greater comprehension.

To believe is more than a particular mode of knowledge; it is a spiritual attitude that determines the life of the believer. Gathering the essential elements of what we have seen so far, Joseph Ratzinger states:

> [Belief] is a human way of taking up a stand in the totality of reality, a way that cannot be reduced to knowledge and is incommensurable with knowledge; it is the bestowal of meaning without which the totality of man would remain homeless, on which man's calculations and actions are based, and without which in the last resort he could not calculate and act, because he can only do this in the context of a meaning that bears him up.[47]

Having looked at faith as a free gift from God and as our concrete response to that gift, we arrive

---

[45] See Ratzinger, *Introduction to Christianity*, 74.

[46] Ratzinger, *A Turning Point for Europe?*, 110.

[47] Ratzinger, *Introduction to Christianity*, 72.

at an understanding of the change that the act of believing entails: to see life in a different way, to be open to conversion, to take on a new attitude toward reality, and to stand firm in the meaning that sustains our life. Based on that understanding, we will look in the next chapter at the act of believing the Christian faith as the act that shapes our personal, integral, and social identities as believers who seek to respond to the free gift we have received and, in so doing, to actualize ourselves fully as human beings.

III. Faith as an Act

Faith, as a free gift from God, awaits our reception in order to bear fruit. Our receiving of the gift of faith, however, is not passive: it is, rather, a true *act* that shapes our identity in at least three respects: it is a personal act, that is, a true relationship with Jesus Christ that is fulfilled in the dynamics of friendship and encounter; it is an integral act, for as humans we can only believe with our whole being; and it is an ecclesial act, insofar as we cannot truly believe unless we are within the community of the Church.

1. FAITH AS A PERSONAL ACT

Having observed the challenges intrinsic to the act of believing as well as those we face in the context of contemporary life (Chapter 1), and having reflected on faith as a gift of God, given and received, followed by a necessary conversion of our lives (Chapter 2), we now look at what constitutes "the most fundamental feature of Christian faith . . . its personal character."[1]

The gift of faith, in all its richness and depth, is not a mere theory that can be learned by reading, an esoteric knowledge or a gathering of truths waiting to be unveiled, or a law that has to be obeyed. Clearly, it is not something that is based solely on a book: "Faith does not refer simply to a book, which as such would be the sole and final authority for the believer. In the center of the Christian faith stands, not a book, but a person—Jesus Christ."[2]

The meaning that we grasp and in which we remain is a real and living person: Jesus Christ. He is the basis for the personal character of faith; He is the person who has chosen us and called us friends (see John 15:15–16), and in whom faith is experienced as a relationship of friendship. He is the person that goes to meet us and invites us to respond to His call with all of our being, in openness to an experience of personal communion. Jesus Christ is the foundation of the Christian faith, which is why "Christian faith has essentially a personal structure,"[3] being a "supremely personal act"[4] that responds authentically to the human heart.

---

[1] Ratzinger, *Introduction to Christianity*, 79.
[2] Joseph Ratzinger, *On the Way to Jesus Christ*, trans. Michael J. Miller (San Francisco: Ignatius Press, 2005), 151.
[3] Ratzinger, *A Turning Point for Europe?*, 115.
[4] Ratzinger, *Gospel, Catechesis, Catechism*, 25.

Jesus Christ as the Foundation of the Personal Nature of Faith

The act of Christian faith has an essentially tangible character that, as we saw earlier, constitutes perhaps the most serious challenge for those who take the leap of faith: to believe "that the fate of all history, our fate, depends on one individual: Jesus of Nazareth."[5]

By believing that everything depends on one individual man, Jesus of Nazareth, the Christian faith affirms its originality in the context of the history of religions, and at the same time, its greatest challenge: the eminently personal character of faith. This maintains that "only the absolute" is God, but at the same time this absolute has the characteristic of being "relative," Creator and revealer, or as previous tradition says, "Person."[6] God is not an abstract idea, an eternal spirit far from us, an impersonal first mover: God is a personal being.

The name of God manifests His personal being: "God has a name, and God calls us by our name. He is a Person, and He seeks the person. He has a heart, and He seeks our heart."[7] However, the name of God that was revealed to Moses in the burning bush does not tell us everything. Only in Jesus, in His name as the expression of His person, does God fully com-

---

[5] Ratzinger, *What It Means to Be a Christian*, 59.
[6] Joseph Ratzinger, *The Feast of Faith: Approaches to a Theology of the Liturgy*, trans. Graham Harrison (San Francisco: Ignatius Press, 1986), 22.
[7] Joseph Ratzinger, *The God of Jesus Christ: Meditations on the Triune God*, trans. Brian McNeil (San Francisco: Ignatius Press, 2008), 24.

municate His message about Himself. His name contains the word Yahweh, but adds His mission: *Yeshua*—to save. "'I am who am'—thanks to Jesus, this now means: 'I am the one who saves you.' His being is salvation."[8] This salvation is offered to us in the person of Jesus Christ, through the gift of faith.

The personal dimension of faith remains fully manifested in Jesus Christ. In our relationship with Him, we can understand the depth of a fundamental affirmation by Ratzinger: the central formula of our Christian faith "is not 'I believe in something,' but 'I believe in you.'"[9] As Christians we do not believe in a vague and distant divinity, in some spiritual foundation of the universe, but in God as a real person with whom we have a relationship of true communion and discover the meaning of our lives. Christian faith, thus,

> is the encounter with the man Jesus, and in this encounter it experiences the meaning of the world as a person. In Jesus' life from the Father, in the immediacy and intensity of his converse with him in prayer and, indeed, face to face, he is God's witness, through whom the intangible has become tangible, the distance has drawn near. And further: he is not simply the witness whose evidence we trust . . . he is the presence of the eternal itself in the world.[10]

---

[8] Ratzinger, *The God of Jesus Christ*, 24.
[9] Ratzinger, *Introduction to Christianity*, 79.
[10] Ratzinger, *Introduction to Christianity*, 79.

Needless to say, Jesus Christ is not only a man with a privileged relationship with God. He is God made man, and therefore the full answer to the desire for the infinite that dwells in the human heart; an answer that is both infinite and close. We can see the meaning of the world in His life, as a person whom we can encounter. From this revelation, we can live with faith as the basis for a new existence. We can understand why faith is both "standing firm" and "understanding," and we are dazzled by the newness of this life:

> Thus faith is the finding of a "you" that upholds me and amid all the unfulfilled—and in the last resort unfulfillable—hope of human encounters gives me the promise of an indestructible love that not only longs for eternity but also guarantees it. Christian faith lives on the discovery that not only is there such a thing as objective meaning but that this meaning knows me and loves me, that I can entrust myself to it like the child who knows that everything he may be wondering about is safe in the "you" of his mother. Thus in the last analysis believing, trusting, and loving are one, and all the theses around which belief revolves are only concrete expressions of the all-embracing about-turn, of the assertion "I believe in you"—of the discovery of God in the countenance of the man Jesus of Nazareth.[11]

---

[11] Ratzinger, *Introduction to Christianity*, 80.

This personal dimension of faith frees it from all possible refuge in limited theories and brings it to the realm of confidence. To say, "I believe," means to say, "'I trust you,' or even as much as 'I rely upon you.'"[12] This also gives faith the simplicity that wells up from love and gives us the fundamental certainty for living, even in the midst of difficulties. "There will be moments in life when, in all kinds of gloom and darkness, faith falls back upon the simple, 'Yes, I believe you, Jesus of Nazareth; I believe that in you was revealed that divine purpose which allows me to live with confidence, tranquility, patience, and courage.'"[13] It bears repeating that we do not believe that faith is easy or that everything will always be clear to our senses. We believe because we trust, and from that trust we accept what is told to us. "As long as this core remains in place, man is living by faith, even if for the moment he finds many of the details of faith obscure and impractical."[14]

Jesus Christ as Logos

The centrality of the "I believe in you" does not imply in any way a denial of believing in the *contents* of the Creed: "Faith is not just a blind gesture, an empty confidence, an adherence to a secret doctrine or the like. On the contrary, it wants to open men's

---

[12] Ratzinger, *Faith and the Future*, 29.

[13] Ratzinger, *Faith and the Future*, 33.

[14] Ratzinger, *Faith and the Future*, 33.

eyes, to open their eyes to truth."[15] The reason for this, Ratzinger declares, is that Christians believe in Jesus Christ who is *Logos*. The one who believes does not throw himself to the irrational, but toward "the *logos*, the *ratio*, toward meaning and so toward truth itself."[16] "The confession of Jesus Christ as *Logos* [Word] means that in him God himself is revealed, the truth of all things."[17]

The understanding of Jesus Christ as *Logos* is of great importance for Ratzinger. Pablo Blanco Sarto maintains that *Logos* is the "geographic center" of *Introduction to Christianity*.[18] Seeing Jesus as *Logos*, Ratzinger connects key concepts for his understanding of faith, such as reason, meaning, love, and person.[19] *Logos* is an essential key to making sense of reality:

---

[15] Ratzinger, *Principles of Catholic Theology*, 337.
[16] Ratzinger, *Introduction to Christianity*, 75.
[17] Ratzinger, *Principles of Catholic Theology*, 338.
[18] See Sarto, *Joseph Ratzinger: Razón y cristianismo*, 77.
[19] *Logos* can be understood as reckoning, measure, proportion, explanation, law, reason, ground, thinking, creative reason, speech, discussion, utterance, wisdom, and of course, word. See *A Greek-English Lexicon*, eds. Henry George Liddell and Robert Scott (Oxford: Oxford University Press, 1990), 1057–1059, and *A Greek-English Lexicon of the New Testament and Other Early Christian Literature. A translation and adaptation of Walter Bauer's Griechisch-Deutsches Wörterbuch zu den Schriften des Neuen Testaments und der übrigen urchristlichen Literatur*, fourth revised and augmented edition, trans. and eds. William F. Arndt and F. Wilbur Gingrich (Cambridge and Chicago: Cambridge University Press and The University of Chicago Press, 1957), 478–480.

> *Logos*, that is, reason, meaning; everything is there: there is a link with reason, a relationship with the meaning (also Christian), since reason, the meaning and Christ are one and the same thing. Rationality and meaning, which are there before and after Christ, adequate to Christ as the whole to the part: He is the all of what was found previously in the universe in separate parts.[20]

Christ as *Logos* thus comes to encounter us, showing that the meaning of the world is not only a truth, but also a person, and even love itself.[21] In reference to the experience of the early Christians expressed in the First Letter of John, "we know and believe the love God has for us," (4:16), Ratzinger expressed in his speech at the University of La Sorbonne in Paris, "Christ had become for these people the discovery of creative love; the rational principle of the universe had revealed itself as love—as that greater reason which accepts into itself even darkness and irrationality and heals them."[22] The meaning *is* love: "Truth and love are identical,"[23] because they are one person. Through relationship with Christ we discover this fundamental truth of reality. That is why the Christian faith today, as always, is based on the

---

[20] Joseph Ratzinger, "Über Zeitgemäßheit und Zeitlosigkeit in der Theologie," *Wort und Warheit* 15 (1960): 180. Cited in Sarto, *Joseph Ratzinger: Razón y cristianismo*, 69 (my translation).

[21] See Ratzinger, *Introduction to Christianity*, 79.

[22] Ratzinger, *Truth and Tolerance*, 155–156.

[23] Ratzinger, *Truth and Tolerance*, 231.

fact that "love and reason [come] together as the two pillars of reality: true reason is love, and love is true reason. They are in their unity the true basis and the goal of all reality."[24] The last word about reality is not an unnamed principle, chaos, or fate, but rather love that is made manifest in the person of Jesus Christ.

The text of the prologue of the Gospel of John is an important key for the comprehension of this mystery: "In the beginning was the Word [*Logos*]" (John 1:1). Ratzinger says that the *Logos* is "the rational origin of all reality, the creative reason from which the world came forth and which is reflected in the world."[25] But there is more: "The Christian faith in God tells us also that God—eternal Reason—is Love."[26] Thus we can understand the internal structure of reality: the *Logos*, as creative reason, gives an internal *logic* to all created beings, a logic that comes from Him, and as such, can only be a logic of love and truth, which constitutes the key for the realization of the world according to its original meaning. This springs from the essence of the Christian faith, because "he whom we believe is not just any man but the Logos, the Word of God, in whom is contained the meaning of the world—its truth."[27]

We find our foundation in the discovery of Christ as *Logos*. Faith brings us to encounter the true life that we desire: "The summit of life is reached only at the

---

[24] Ratzinger, *Truth and Tolerance*, 183.
[25] Joseph Ratzinger, *Europe: Today and Tomorrow*, trans. Michael J. Miller (San Francisco: Ignatius Press, 2007), 97.
[26] Ratzinger, *Europe: Today and Tomorrow*, 97.
[27] Ratzinger, *Principles of Catholic Theology*, 337.

place where other things are found: knowledge and love . . . a knowledge that becomes love and love that comes from knowledge and leads to knowledge."[28] Thanks to this encounter with Christ, an experience of knowledge and love, we arrive at "the basic understanding in which we become aware of our foundation, we learn to accept it, and because we have a foundation we are able to live."[29]

Faith as Encounter and Friendship

Now we must consider the relational aspect of the faith. The Christian faith does not consist of learning facts or building theoretical systems, but rather in welcoming a Person and accepting what He teaches. Faith comes through an encounter with that Person and the experience of His friendship.

Encounter with Christ and Freedom

The gift of faith, as we have seen, is received through an act of conversion. But conversion to what? What is the reason and the goal of conversion? *Metánoia* (conversion) is the act of opening ourselves to the truth in which we stand; it allows us to accept the newness of a reasonable and loving foundation of reality. However, the foundation is not abstract or un-

---

[28] Ratzinger et al., *Handing on the Faith*, 26.
[29] Ratzinger et al., *Handing on the Faith*, 26–27.

reachable, but rather it is the love that we see in the person of Christ, who is the meaning of the world. That is why we can only accept this vision of reality if we have a personal encounter with the Lord Jesus. As Ratzinger says, "we cannot perform this act without touching our deepest ground, the living God who is present in the depths of our existence as its sustaining foundation."[30]

Faith is encounter. It is a deeply personal act: "[I]t is the answer of a person to a personal call."[31] In that respect, it is important to note that Ratzinger's approach differs from those who say that the being of the believer is diluted in God.[32] For Ratzinger, the Christian faith requires that the identity of the believer remain present and that the distinction between the "I" and the "you" is not lost or diminished. Rather, "over against the unity of merging, with its tendency to eliminate identity, should be set personal experience: unity of love is higher than formless identity."[33] The differences not only remain, but also become "the means to a higher unity."[34]

The Trinitarian foundation of this new way is revealed in Christ: "[I]t is the union of love, in which the differences are not destroyed, but are transformed into a higher union of those who love each other, just as it

---

[30] Ratzinger, *Gospel, Catechesis, Catechism*, 25.

[31] Ratzinger, *A Turning Point for Europe?*, 115.

[32] See Ratzinger, *Truth and Tolerance*, 34.

[33] Ratzinger, *Truth and Tolerance*, 47.

[34] Joseph Ratzinger, "The Theology of the Liturgy," in Joseph Ratzinger et al., *Looking Again at the Question of the Liturgy with Cardinal Ratzinger*, ed. Alcuin Reid (Farnborough: Saint Michael's Abbey Press, 2003), 26.

is found, as in an archetype, in the Trinitarian union of God."[35] This union of love is achieved through the encounter between one who seeks and one who responds. Therefore, the nature of this encounter is of great importance for Ratzinger's vision of the faith.

This is why freedom is essential for belief. God initiates an encounter with man but always respects his liberty. We must open the door to God (see Rev 3:20) for the act of faith to take place. God, from His infinite freedom and love, looks at us and gives the gift of faith; we, from the freedom we have received, welcome the gift and the new life it brings.

The freedom involved in the act of faith carries with it the risk that the gift may be refused. The logic of the free love that the faith puts forth means that God has "unconditional respect for the freedom of his creature[s]."[36] God comes to meet us in every moment, but "never, in any case, forces anyone to be saved. God accepts man's freedom . . . Even on account of the unconditional greatness of God's love—indeed, because of that very quality—the freedom to refuse, and thus the possibility of perdition, is not removed."[37] This reality of liberty—including the risk that comes with it—should cause us to think of the responsibility of our response and so also, of the seriousness and grandeur of our life:

---

[35] Ratzinger, "The Theology of the Liturgy," 26.

[36] Joseph Ratzinger, *Eschatology: Death and Eternal Life*, trans. Michael Waldstein (Washington, DC: The Catholic University of America Press, 1988), 215.

[37] Joseph Ratzinger, *God Is Near Us: The Eucharist, the Heart of Life*, trans. Henry Taylor (San Francisco: Ignatius Press, 2003), 36–37.

"[T]he specificity of Christianity is shown in this conviction of the greatness of man. Human life is fully serious . . . the Christian man or woman must live with such seriousness and be aware of it. It is a seriousness which takes on tangible form in the Cross of Christ."[38]

Christ as *Logos* is the foundation of liberty: "Faith, which knows the Logos as the beginning, has the primacy of freedom as its starting point. Only the link to the Logos guarantees freedom as the structural principle of what really exists."[39] Liberty is also a structural principle of the act of faith; the various elements of faith are ordered by the liberty that accepts the gift. That is why Ratzinger says that "Christian faith in its essence includes a comprehensive philosophy of freedom."[40] We see this expressed in a most profound way in prayer, the deep realm where the believer communicates with God. Christian prayer "is the response one freedom makes to another freedom, an encounter of love."[41] The loving encounter of faith that is manifested in prayer demands a double exodus, that of God and that of man. Both go out of themselves to freely meet in the context of faith. As we read in the *Catechism of the Catholic Church*: "Whether we realize it or not, prayer is the encounter of God's thirst with ours. God thirsts that we may thirst for him" (CCC 2560).

---

[38] Ratzinger, *Eschatology*, 216–217.
[39] Ratzinger, *A Turning Point for Europe?*, 115–116.
[40] Ratzinger, *A Turning Point for Europe?*, 115.
[41] Ratzinger, *A Turning Point for Europe?*, 116.

Faith as Friendship

The encounter that allows us to have faith is developed as a loving relationship between two persons in the specific form of friendship. Faith is not a blind or theoretical acceptance of certain facts, nor the mere compliance with a set of rules, but instead a true experience of friendship. Indeed, friendship is the form of the new covenant of God with His people, sealed in the Last Supper: "[I]t is not a contract with conditions but the gift of friendship, irrevocably bestowed. Instead of law, we have grace."[42] This is why faith cannot be seen as the last resort in the face of the failure of every other option. Far from that, "faith in God is a positive act of love and trust, of conversion, of renewal of life, and something like that cannot simply rise from a failed experience, from an emptiness . . . it requires a positive experience, that is the value of a love that is given to God."[43]

The Christian faith is lived tangibly as love in the beautiful form of friendship. At the beginning of the 2005 conclave, in his last homily before being elected Successor of Peter, Ratzinger explained in a profound and beautiful way the friendship of Jesus Christ, in reference to the discourse in the fifteenth chapter of the Gospel of John. There Jesus explains friendship in two ways. The first is that of trust and knowledge:

---

[42] Joseph Ratzinger, *Many Religions—One Covenant: Israel, the Church and the World*, trans. Graham Harrison (San Francisco: Ignatius Press, 1999), 67.

[43] Joseph Ratzinger, *Ser Cristiano en la Era Neopagana* [To be a Christian in a neopagan era] (Madrid: Encuentro, 1995), 145 (my translation).

There are no secrets between friends: Christ tells us all that he hears from the Father; he gives us his full trust and with trust, also knowledge. He reveals his face and his heart to us. He shows us the tenderness he feels for us, his passionate love that goes even as far as the folly of the Cross. He entrusts himself to us, he gives us the power to speak in his name: "this is my body . . . ," "I forgive you . . . ," He entrusts his Body, the Church, to us.[44]

Jesus entrusts His disciples with the secrets of His heart, making them not only His servants, but His friends. The second aspect of this friendship is the "communion of wills":

Idem velle—idem nolle [same desires—same dislikes] was also for Romans the definition of friendship. "You are my friends if you do what I command you" (Jn 15:14). Friendship with Christ coincides with the third request of the Our Father: "Thy will be done on earth as it is in heaven." At his hour in the Garden of Gethsemane, Jesus transformed our rebellious human will into a will conformed and united with the divine will. He suffered the whole drama of our autonomy—and precisely by placing our will in God's hands, he gives us true freedom: "Not as I will, but as you will" (Mt 26:39).

---

[44] Ratzinger, Homily at the Mass "Pro Eligendo Romano Pontifice."

> Our redemption is brought about in this communion of wills: being friends of Jesus, to become friends of God. The more we love Jesus, the more we know him, the more our true freedom develops and our joy in being redeemed flourishes. Thank you, Jesus, for your friendship![45]

An authentic vision of the act of faith as friendship will clear up all false ideas between our freedom and God's, between His plan and ours. Obedience is then understood as the natural consequence of the one who loves and believes. Therefore, Ratzinger says, "faith is obedience; it means that we relearn the essential form of our being—our nature as creatures—and in this way become authentic."[46]

This concrete experience of love contained in believing is a reality that fills our existence with life. In effect, faith is life, because it is a relationship,[47] because it is dialogue and confidence. In faith, we accept the love of God and seek to embrace it in our lives: "[M]an's response to the God who is good to him is love, and loving God means worshipping him."[48] This all-important adoration brings joy and

---

[45] Ratzinger, Homily at the Mass "Pro Eligendo Romano Pontifice."

[46] Joseph Ratzinger, *A New Song for the Lord: Faith in Christ and Liturgy Today*, trans. Martha M. Matesich (New York: Crossroad, 1997), 49.

[47] Ratzinger et al., *Handing on the Faith*, 26.

[48] Joseph Ratzinger, *The Spirit of the Liturgy*, trans. John Saward, in Joseph Ratzinger, *Collected Works*, vol. 11, *Theology of the Liturgy: The Sacramental Foundation of Christian*

fullness that could never be acquired on our own and unveils all illusion through the authentic love that we see on the Cross: "Life is worth living. This is the *evangelium*. This is why, even as the message of the Cross, it is glad tidings for one who believes; the only glad tidings is that Christianity is, by its very nature, joy—the ability to be joyful. The χαιρε: 'Rejoice!' with which it begins expresses its whole nature."[49]

2. FAITH AS AN INTEGRAL ACT

In looking at faith as a personal act, we saw its relational aspect as a free encounter with Christ that brings life and joy to the believer. This personal relationship involves the whole being of the believer and is therefore also an integral act that involves our reason, sentiment, and will, an act which we can experience and verify in our daily life.

Reason, Sentiment, and Will

As we have seen, Ratzinger's approach to the act of faith leads to a synthetic view, which avoids false contradictions: he presents faith as gift given and received, as personal communion and content, and as objective and subjective knowledge. Similarly, we will now see

---

Existence, ed. Michael J. Miller (San Francisco: Ignatius Press, 2014), 14.

[49] Ratzinger, *Principles of Catholic Theology*, 81.

that he presents faith not as an act that pertains to only one dimension of our being, perhaps even to the detriment of others, but as a living reality that "demands our whole existence, our will, our love."[50]

This view of faith as an integral act responds to the unique structure of the Christian faith. "Believing is not an act of the understanding alone, not simply an act of the will, not just an act of feeling, but an act in which all the spiritual powers of man are at work together."[51] It is "an orientation of our existence as a whole . . . faith is not a merely intellectual, or merely volitional, or merely emotional activity—it is all of these things together."[52]

The spiritual structure of faith helps us to understand the integrity and personal intensity that the act of faith demands of us—an act that causes us to adhere to and accept God and His primacy. That is why "an essential part of our faith in the one God is the acknowledgment of God's will. Worship of God is not only a sinking into him: it also gives us back to ourselves, it challenges us in the midst of our everyday lives, summoning all the powers of our mind, feeling, and will."[53]

Reason

Joseph Ratzinger insists that belief does not mean giving ourselves over to the irrational,[54] nor is it a

---

[50] Ratzinger, *God and the World*, 36.

[51] Ratzinger, *Pilgrim Fellowship of Faith*, 24.

[52] Ratzinger, *Gospel, Catechesis, Catechism*, 24.

[53] Ratzinger, *Many Religions—One Covenant*, 100.

[54] Ratzinger, *Introduction to Christianity*, 53.

"resignation of reason in view of the limits of our knowledge."[55] Faith is an option that does not go against reason.

In the act of believing, listening is a priority. Faith is not a product of our own thoughts, but instead a gift that comes from outside ourselves. From this gift and through listening we are then able to understand that "the essence of faith, however, is that I do not meet with something that has been thought up, but that here something meets me that is greater than anything we can think of for ourselves."[56] This rethinking is a constant movement looking for greater understanding: "[B]elieving is a pilgrimage of thought, which is still following the way."[57] Thought is not passively still and quiet, but "is still reflecting and is still in a state of seeking"[58]—it aims to arrive at the truth.

In this sense, it is illuminating to see the place that Ratzinger gives to Christian faith in the context of world religions and the search for truth about God. Clearly, from its origins, Christianity has rejected Gnosticism and other forms of closed thinking, unmistakably opting for reason and universality. In the context of other religions, Christianity has always understood itself as a religion of reason, and not as an irrational approach to the divine.[59] Within

---

[55] Ratzinger, *A Turning Point for Europe?*, 110.
[56] Joseph Ratzinger, *Storia e dogma* [History and dogma] (Milan: Jaca Book, 1993), 43, cited in Sarto, *Joseph Ratzinger: Razón y cristianismo*, 108 (my translation).
[57] Ratzinger, *Pilgrim Fellowship of Faith*, 25.
[58] Ratzinger, *Pilgrim Fellowship of Faith*, 25.
[59] See Ratzinger, "Europe in the Crisis of Cultures," 353.

the context of cultural and religious relativism, the "Christian faith has proved to be the most universal and rational religious culture."[60]

Ratzinger tells about the dispute between St. Augustine and Marcus Terentius Varro (the most learned among Romans, according to Seneca), who proposed the existence of three great types of theology: the mythical (related to poetry), the civil (related to politics), and the physical (related to philosophy). Augustine significantly placed Christianity in the arena of physical theology, in the sphere of philosophical enlightenment.[61] In doing this, he places himself completely in continuity with the early Christian theologians and with St. Paul:

> What that means is the Christian faith is not based on poetry and politics, the two great sources of religion; it is based on knowledge . . . . In Christianity, enlightenment has become part of religion and is no longer its opponent. Because that is how it was, because Christianity saw itself as embodying the victory of demythologization, the victory of knowledge, and with that the victory of truth, it necessarily regarded itself as universal and had to be carried to all peoples.[62]

This affirmation of Christianity as the *religio*

---

[60] Joseph Ratzinger, *Values in a Time of Upheaval*, trans. Brian McNeil (New York: Crossroad, 2006), 69.

[61] See Ratzinger, *Truth and Tolerance*, 169.

[62] Ratzinger, *Truth and Tolerance*, 170.

vera (true religion) helps us understand that there is no contradiction between the philosophical vision of God and His biblical image. In fact, "the Christian faith in God accepts in itself the philosophical doctrine of God and embraces it."[63] Moreover, "if we distinguish too closely between the God of faith and the God of the philosophers, we deprive faith of its objectivity."[64] Thus, assuming the intuitions of the philosophers about God, Christianity offers a religion of truth, not by the common claim of all religions of being in the right, but because the basis of the Christian faith is Jesus Christ, the *Logos*, the meaning and truth of the universe. In that way we can say not only that the Christian faith is rational, but also meta-rational; it takes reason to an even higher plane, to the space in which *Logos* expresses truth and becomes the new principle from which we approach life. In Christ, who is love and truth, and thus the meaning of reality, we appreciate the harmony of faith and reason, both needed, mutually reinforcing one another. "By no means the least important practical function of faith is to offer healing for the reason as reason . . . to bring it to itself again."[65] And at the same time, reason gives life to faith: "[W]ithout faith, philosophy cannot be whole, but faith without reason cannot be human."[66]

---

[63] Joseph Ratzinger, *El Dios de la fe y el Dios de los filósofos* [The God of faith and the faith of the philosophers] (Madrid: Taurus, 1960), 18–19, cited in Sarto, *Joseph Ratzinger: Razón y cristianismo*, 61 (my translation).

[64] Ratzinger, *Principles of Catholic Theology*, 73.

[65] Ratzinger, *Truth and Tolerance*, 136.

[66] Ratzinger, *Truth and Tolerance*, 136.

Sentiment

Faith also responds to the sentimental dimension of the human being. It is not just a cold meaning grasped at by reason, bringing it to a theoretical truth, but something that is warmly welcomed with all of the energies of the heart. Faith informs reason with revealed truth, and in turn it ought to move the person's sentiments and affections if it is meant to be lived out in a truly human way.

The importance of the sentimental aspect of faith is not difficult to perceive, even for unbelievers. But this dimension must be properly understood. In modern thought, this aspect of faith is often emphasized to a point where faith loses its objective foundation. At the Sorbonne, then-Cardinal Ratzinger began a lecture on the truth of Christianity by making reference to the division between the objective-scientific and the subjective-religious, proposed by Max Planck[67] as the key for the harmonic coexistence between science and religion. Ratzinger summarized this view: "In natural science it was a matter of things being true or false; in religion, of their being good or bad, valuable or worthless. The two realms were quite separate, belonging to the objective and the subjective aspects of the world."[68] For proponents of this view, the validity of religion can be recognized if its value is limited to the realm of the subjective.

---

[67] Max Planck (1858–1947) was a German theoretical physicist and the originator of the quantum theory. He received the Nobel Prize in 1918.

[68] Ratzinger, *Truth and Tolerance*, 138.

At the root of this approach to faith and religion is the influence of Friedrich Schleiermacher,[69] who, trying to rescue religion from the attacks of the Enlightenment, wanted to give it a new momentum by obtaining for it independence and autonomy in relation to the other areas of knowledge. This independence would come from a rigid separation among reason, will, and sentiment as the areas or "the three provinces of the human mind, and none is derived from any other, and none can be transmuted into any other. The understanding is correlated to science, the will to ethics, emotion [sentiment] to religion, which he defined as beholding and sensing the universe or as sensitivity to and appreciation of the infinite."[70] Thus, faith comes to be pure sentiment and remains as an area of the subjective, removed from reason and will, for all three would then be mutually independent.

It is not difficult to see the influence that this approach has in our time. However, it is also not difficult to see that the separation between the scientific-rational-objective and the religious-sentimental-subjective does not correspond to human nature or to the nature of faith. Werner Heisenberg[71] expressed his uneasiness about this proposal, saying, "I have to admit, that I do not feel happy about this division. I doubt whether any human society can in

---

[69] Friedrich Schleiermacher (1768–1834) was a German philosopher and theologian, known for his efforts to reconcile the Enlightenment with Protestantism.

[70] Ratzinger, *Faith and the Future*, 63.

[71] Werner Heisenberg (1901–1976) was a German theoretical physicist; he was awarded the Nobel Prize in Physics in 1932 for the creation of quantum mechanics.

the long term live with this sharp division between knowledge and faith."[72]

Faith is not pure sentiment. Faith ought to reach beyond the realm of reason, thus assuming through a personal act of trust and friendship with Christ the sentiments and affections that adhere to Him who is love and truth. The human being open to the infinite finds in faith a personal and objective sustenance, and receives the possibility of finding a way of warmly welcoming what reason accepts as certain.

In the search for balance between reason and sentiment in the act of believing, Ratzinger suggests Marian piety as a key to harmony: "The affirmation of Mary's motherhood and the affirmation of her representation of the Church are related as *factum* and *mysterium facti*, as the fact and the sense that gives the fact its meaning. The two things are inseparable: the fact without its sense would be blind; the sense without the fact would be empty."[73] In the midst of the tendency to excessively separate faith from reason, sentiment from will, and in view of the danger of relegating faith and religion to a mere sentimentality without basis, a filial affection for Mary helps "to awaken the heart and to purify it in faith."[74] Sen-

---

[72] Werner Heisenberg, *Der Teil und das Ganze: Gespräche im Umkreis der Atomphysik* (Munich: R. Piper, 1969), 117, cited in Ratzinger, *Truth and Tolerance*, 139.

[73] Joseph Ratzinger, "Thoughts on the Place of Marian Doctrine and Piety in Faith and Theology as a Whole," in Joseph Ratzinger and Hans Urs von Balthasar, *Mary: The Church at the Source* (San Francisco: Ignatius Press, 2005), 30.

[74] Ratzinger, "Thoughts on the Place of Marian Doctrine," 36.

timents have their proper place in the act of faith, a place defined by faith, directed by reason, and bound by will.

Will

Faith does not remain in reason or in sentiments, but is solidified through the will through concrete actions of daily life. The act of faith is truly integral: it welcomes with the mind a meaning of the world that is truth and love, adheres to it with affection and sentiment, and lives according to what it believes through the will.

We can find two ways of understanding the role that the will plays in the act of believing, according to Joseph Ratzinger. First, approximating the essence of the Christian faith from a text of Thomas Aquinas, he defines faith as "thinking with assent."[75] In faith there is the conjunction of thinking and consenting, which is common to the sciences. In the sciences, consent is a consequence of thinking: it is affirmed because it has been thought. However, in faith, the relationship between thinking and consent is different: "[I]n the act of believing the assent comes about in a way that is different from the way in which it comes about in the act of knowing: not through the degree of evidence bringing the process of thought to its conclusion, but by an act of will, in connection with which the thought process remains open and still under way."[76] How is

---

[75] Ratzinger, *Pilgrim Fellowship of Faith*, 21.
[76] Ratzinger, *Pilgrim Fellowship of Faith*, 22.

that possible? "We are able to give the assent of faith because the will—the heart—has been touched by God, 'affected' by him. Through being touched in this way, the will knows that even what is still not 'clear' to the reason is true."[77]

The second way of understanding the role of the will in believing is what we commonly understand as the practical aspect of faith: that of living it out in daily life. "Faith is not pure theory, it is 'a pilgrimage,' that is, a *praxis*."[78] What we believe has consequences in daily life; moreover, we believe authentically if we live according to what has been accepted by reason and received by our sentiments. To believe is not simply to accept interesting ideas or experience intense sentiments. On the contrary, faith brings new convictions that "have an immediate practical content. Faith includes morality, not simply generic ideals. It gives rather concrete guidance for human life."[79]

Of course, we need not establish false contradictions or mutually exclusive emphases. To overemphasize the will when considering faith is dangerous. Activism is a distortion that proposes that what truly matters in faith is action. It goes hand in hand with what some have proposed as the priority of *orthopraxis* (right action) above *orthodoxy* (right doctrine).[80] Ac-

---

[77] Ratzinger, *Pilgrim Fellowship of Faith*, 23. "Heart," in biblical language, is what St. Thomas uses to refer to will.

[78] Joseph Ratzinger, *La Fe como camino: Contribución al ethos cristiano en el momento actual* [Faith as a road: Contributions to Christian ethics in the present moment] (Barcelona: Ediciones Internacionales Universitarias, 1997), 55 (my translation).

[79] Joseph Ratzinger, *La Fe como camino*, 55.

[80] Ratzinger, *Truth and Tolerance*, 122–126.

tivism is always a temptation, considering the urgency of the needs of the world, but it is a sign of lack of faith in God. In a text about creation, while speaking of the importance of the Third Commandment, Ratzinger says that when denying the rest of God, the chosen people fell into slavery: "The people had rejected God's rest, its leisure, its worship, its peace, its freedom, and so they fell into the slavery of activity."[81] Action, in itself, can be a "place" of faith, in which we are united with Him whom we welcome with our mind and affections. Through our action, the will attaches itself to what reason and sentiment have received, and through living, believes. Only through daily coherence with the gift of faith does our action become authentic and integral, and Christianity acquires its internal vigor, thanks to "the connection of faith with reason and by directing behavior by *caritas*."[82]

Experience and the Knowledge of Faith

Having shown that the act of faith is a "personal act" that involves the entirety of the person—reason, sentiment, and will—we now ask how is the act of faith realized in the complex nature of a human being?

For Ratzinger, the fundamental point of departure for understanding how belief is realized in man is the Aristotelian axiom that St. Thomas formulated

---

[81] Joseph Ratzinger, *In the Beginning: A Catholic Understanding of the Story of Creation and the Fall*, trans. Boniface Ramsey, OP (Grand Rapids, MI: Eerdmans, 1995), 32.

[82] Ratzinger, *Truth and Tolerance*, 174.

as *Nihil est in intellectu quod non prius fuerit in sensu* (there is nothing in the intellect that was not first in the senses).[83] The senses are the door through which all human knowledge must pass, and it is in the experience of sense perception that knowledge begins. St. Thomas expands upon this Aristotelian principle when he affirms "that we cannot know God except through the senses and that even our way of thinking about God is dependent on and mediated by sense perception."[84]

This conclusion from a philosophical premise is confirmed if we look at the "pedagogical method of Holy Scripture"[85] used by Jesus: the parables. Ratzinger gives great importance to the parables as a pathway to the knowledge of God: "[T]he parable is the way in which knowledge of faith is to be realized in this world (Jn 16:25) . . . the parable appears as the structure by which access is to be had to the mystery of the kingdom of God."[86] The parables transcend the world of creation by drawing us to the Creator, taking us through the historical experience of faith, and giving us the way to interpret daily life.[87] Through parables we see that "the content of faith is made transparent in the reality of the senses, and this knowledge of the faith has, in its turn, a reciprocal effect on the world of the senses, making it comprehensible as a movement that transcends itself."[88]

---

[83] Ratzinger, *Principles of Catholic Theology*, 343–345.
[84] Ratzinger, *Principles of Catholic Theology*, 344.
[85] Ratzinger, *Principles of Catholic Theology*, 344.
[86] Ratzinger, *Principles of Catholic Theology*, 344.
[87] Ratzinger, *Principles of Catholic Theology*, 344.
[88] Ratzinger, *Principles of Catholic Theology*, 344–345.

While the fact that knowledge of the faith proceeds from the experience of the senses retains all its validity, it is also true that faith does not remain there. Echoing the famous dictum of St. Ignatius of Loyola *"Deus semper maior"* (God is always greater), Ratzinger affirms that God is always beyond what we are able to grasp of Him simply through our experience: "The always greater God can be known only in the transcendence of the always 'more,' in the constant revision of our experiences. Thus faith and experience form the continuum of a road that must go farther and farther."[89] The experience of the senses is an indispensable entry for the act of faith, but that only happens if faith is given more importance than experience: "Faith starts with experience but it cannot be limited by any experience that happens to present itself."[90] Believing always assumes and yet also surpasses our experiences, for it demands that we go out of ourselves in openness to what we receive from God. As such, faith is a knowledge that is realized in accord with the nature of God, who being "pure relatedness"[91] as Trinity, is an active communion of persons that go out of themselves in love.

This type of knowledge of faith depends on both God and man. From here we find another unique characteristic: the objective dimension joined with the subjective: "The Christian God is not just reason,

---

[89] Ratzinger, *Principles of Catholic Theology*, 346.
[90] Ratzinger, *Principles of Catholic Theology*, 346.
[91] Joseph Ratzinger, "Reviving the Tradition: Concerning the Notion of Person in Theology," *Communio* 17 (Fall 1990): 447.

objective meaning, the geometry of the universe, but he is speech, relation, Word, and Love. He is sighted reason, which sees and hears, which can be called upon and has a personal character."[92] A unique type of knowledge of faith is based on this union of meaning and love in the person of Jesus Christ, one that comes from the fact that "the 'objective' meaning of the world is a subject, in relation to me."[93] The objectivity of the faith is based on the person of Jesus Christ as *Logos*, as truth and love. That is why the nature of the knowledge of faith is totally unique; it is about a very personal knowledge which, at the same time, is very objective.[94]

Knowledge of faith is not a collection of scientific facts arrived at by investigation, nor does believing mean collecting facts about God and using them to build a system: "Faith is not primarily a colossal edifice of numerous supernatural facts, standing like a curious second order of knowledge alongside the realm of science, but an assent to God, who gives us hope and confidence."[95] This truth is liberating, since we do not believe only from what we build with our limited understanding, but rather from what we receive as a greater gift to which we adhere. And while the act of faith as personal adherence is not in any way in contradiction to the contents of our faith, Ratzinger does hold that

---

[92] Joseph Ratzinger, *Dogma and Preaching: Applying Christian Doctrine to Daily Life*, trans. Michael J. Miller and Matthew J. O'Connell (San Francisco: Ignatius Press, 2011), 94.

[93] Ratzinger, *Dogma and Preaching*, 94.

[94] See Ratzinger, *Principles of Catholic Theology*, 72.

[95] Ratzinger, *Faith and the Future*, 30.

there is a priority in our believing: "[T]he assent of faith as such is concerned with the whole, and only secondarily has it to do with the part, with the separate contents to which faith assents."[96] Therefore, the assent of faith is a priority insofar as it is an act: we choose to believe in Jesus Christ and by believing in *Him* we believe in *what* He reveals: "What's essential about Christ himself is not that he proclaimed certain ideas—which, of course, he also did. Rather, I become a Christian by believing in this event. God stepped into the world and acted; so it is an action, a reality, not only an intellectual entity."[97] In a new way we see the richness and completeness that characterizes and distinguishes the act of Christian faith: "Faith, as the New Testament understands it, is more than a fundamental trust; it is my Yes to a content that compels my belief."[98] Faith and content, objectivity and subjectivity, reason and love—everything is reconciled and unified in the person of Jesus Christ, true God and true man. He allows us to believe by sharing His own vision: "Christian faith is sharing in the vision of Jesus, mediated by his word, which is the authentic expression of his vision. Jesus' vision is the point of reference of our faith, the point where it is anchored in reality."[99] We do not see by ourselves what we would never be able see; "the act of faith . . . is a sharing in

---

[96] Ratzinger, *Faith and the Future*, 32.
[97] Joseph Ratzinger, *Salt of the Earth: The Church at the End of the Millennium: An Interview with Peter Seewald*, trans. Adrian Walker (San Francisco: Ignatius Press, 1997), 20.
[98] Ratzinger, *Principles of Catholic Theology*, 337.
[99] Ratzinger, *To Look on Christ*, 32.

the vision of Jesus, propping oneself up on Jesus."[100] Through what He has seen, as eternal Son become man, we can enter and see what He has revealed to us.

Finally, the act of faith is not an isolated choice that happens only once, but a constant process, a path that is not uniform or pre-determined: "Because [faith] is so closely connected with our life that moves up and down in all sorts of ways, there are always setbacks that require a new start."[101] Faith is life, a relationship, and its knowledge depends on divine revelation that comes to each believer. Because of this, faith participates in the instability that we find in our path through life. However, it is an instability anchored in a certainty that is verified as we advance along the way: "In the life of faith a certain evidence of this faith is growing: its reality affects us, and the experience of a life lived in faith verifies the fact for us that Jesus is indeed the savior of the world."[102] Our belief is verified to the extent that we experience again and again, and hopefully each time with more certainty, that the meaning of the world is love and that Jesus Christ is the *Logos* in which we live. In that way, we see that "only the experience of God can yield knowledge of God."[103]

---

[100] Ratzinger, *To Look on Christ*, 37.
[101] Ratzinger, *To Look on Christ*, 34.
[102] Ratzinger, *To Look on Christ*, 35.
[103] Ratzinger, *Principles of Catholic Theology*, 360.

3. FAITH AS AN ECCLESIAL ACT

The personal and integral aspects of the act of faith are both characteristics belonging to a vision that is principally oriented toward encountering and accepting Jesus Christ, believing in Him with all our being. The third aspect has to do with the communal character of faith: the act of faith as an ecclesial act. As we have seen, we do not believe because we have seen on our own; faith is participation, above all, in the vision of Jesus. This vision of Jesus becomes accessible through the experience of other believers, in particular that of the saints: "The saints, as the living personifications of faith actually experienced and tested, of a transcendence actually experienced and confirmed, are themselves, we might say, places into which one can enter, in which faith as experience has been, as it were, stored, anthropologically seasoned and brought near to our own lives."[104] In the lives of the saints we can see faith realized through their experience and also in their testimonies and words. This is also true for the science of faith: theology. Following St. Thomas Aquinas, Ratzinger says that "theology too is a 'subordinate science,' which does not itself 'see' and 'prove' its ultimate rational foundations. It is as it were suspended from the 'knowledge of the saints.'"[105] That is why Ratzinger insists that we are secondhand believers. Faith at its beginning is taken from the experience of others that help

---

[104] Ratzinger, *Principles of Catholic Theology*, 352.
[105] Ratzinger, *To Look on Christ*, 33.

us to believe when we do not yet see well; it is a vital confidence and security that opens the road that takes us to a deep dimension of faith.[106] And, even as we mature in our faith, we never cease to lean on the experience of those who, in some way, transmit the light of faith with their lives: faith is never a purely individual act; to believe we always need others. It is from here that we understand the importance of the ecclesial aspect of the act of believing.

The Symbol and the Dialogical Structure of Faith

We can appreciate the ecclesial dimension of the act of faith in light of the Creed, a text that has its origin in ritual, namely, the baptismal liturgy. Its most primitive formula is a dialogue: a triple question and answer. These elements reveal an important truth about the faith: "[I]n the prehistory of this confession and in its original form, the whole anthropological shape of belief is present as well."[107] This anthropological form of the faith refers to its structure as a dialogue: the complementary character between the personal and the social aspects of believing: "It becomes evident that belief is not the result of lonely meditation in which the 'I,' freed from all ties and reflecting alone on the truth, thinks something out for itself; on the contrary, it is the result of a dialogue, the expression of a hearing, receiving, and

---

[106] Ratzinger, *Principles of Catholic Theology*, 352.
[107] Ratzinger, *Introduction to Christianity*, 90.

answering that guides man through the exchanges of 'I' and 'You' to the 'We' of those who all believe in the same way."[108]

In this we find a significant difference between faith and philosophy; the latter proceeds from reflection and the former from listening. Faith is not characterized as "the thinking out of something that can be thought out and that at the end of the process is then at my disposal as the result of my thought. On the contrary, it is characteristic of faith that it comes from hearing, that it is the reception of something that I have not thought out, so that in the last analysis thinking in the context of faith is always a thinking over of something previously heard and received."[109] That is why in faith the *word* predominates over the *idea*, and it is essential that the word originates from outside. This is a guarantee of its greatness because it fosters the acceptance of a broader horizon, one that is above all possible thought and only accessible through hearing the newness of the Good News. Authentic faith is only born from a personal invitation and response, the fruit of a dialogue:

> In this process of turning about, as which faith must consequently be understood, the I and the We, the I and the You interact in a way that expresses a whole image of man. On the one side, we have a highly personal process, whose inalienable individuality finds clear expression both in the triple "*I*

---

[108] Ratzinger, *Introduction to Christianity*, 90.
[109] Ratzinger, *Introduction to Christianity*, 91.

believe" and in the triple "*I* renounce" that precedes it: it is *my* existence that must turn here, that is to trans-form itself. But together with this extremely personal element we also find here that the decision of the I is made in answer to a question, in the interplay of "Do you believe?" and "I do believe!"[110]

This nature of faith as an act of dialogue that we find in the Creed is a very important theme in Ratzinger's thought: few theologians have expressed this interweaving of I and You in regards to the faith as insistently and beautifully as he has.[111]

Faith and Communion

Reflection on the Creed, the Symbol of Faith, leads to a consideration of the dimension of communion that belongs to the act of believing. Referring to the Greek origins of the word *symbolon*, Ratzinger says that "man holds the faith only as a *symbolon*, a broken, incomplete piece that can only attain unity and completeness when it is laid together with the others. Only in *symballein*, in fitting together with them, can the *symballein*, the fitting together with God, take place."[112] We cannot believe on our own, nor can we reach God by our own strength. We find ourselves with "a structur-

---

[110] Ratzinger, *Introduction to Christianity*, 88–89.

[111] Regarding this, see Pierre Eyt, "Reflection by Pierre Eyt," in Ratzinger et al., *Handing on the Faith*, 46.

[112] Ratzinger, *Introduction to Christianity*, 98.

al law of biblical faith . . . God comes to men only through men."[113]

Furthermore, this relationship with others is not just instrumental to believing. We do not simply hear the Word proclaimed to us and then go our separate ways. Faith brings us to communion: "Faith, therefore, not only has an I and a Thou, but also a We."[114] We believe with others, in vital and constant communion: "Faith demands unity and calls for the fellow believer; it is by nature related to a Church. A Church is not a secondary organization of ideas, quite out of accordance with them and hence at best a necessary evil; it belongs necessarily to a faith whose significance lies in the interplay of common confession and worship."[115] Indeed, "the Christian experience begins in the ordinary course of communal experience, but it relies, for its future course, on the extent and richness of the experiences already accumulated throughout history by the world of faith."[116]

We then enter into the truth of a central and indispensable aspect of the act of faith: to believe *in* the Church. She is the environment in which we hear the Word resonate and to which we adhere with our whole life; she is the setting in which belief develops: "Faith is no private path to God; it leads into the people of God and into its history."[117] The relationship with God that is born from faith is not

---

[113] Ratzinger, *Faith and the Future*, 44.

[114] Ratzinger et al., *Handing on the Faith*, 27.

[115] Ratzinger, *Introduction to Christianity*, 98.

[116] Ratzinger, *Principles of Catholic Theology*, 350–351.

[117] Ratzinger, *Truth and Tolerance*, 71.

just an isolated, personal matter: "It is something at once wholly interior and yet wholly public."[118] Both dimensions are lived in the Church and not outside of her. In a clear and radical way, there is no faith without the Church:[119] "Faith is necessarily what may be called churchly faith. It lives and moves in the 'we' of the Church, one with the common 'I' of Jesus Christ."[120]

The ecclesial dimension of belief leads us to understand the "social aspect of the phenomenon of faith."[121] We do not believe by ourselves; we need others to know the faith, to accept it, and to live it. It is not a mere functional matter, but a social dimension born from our identity as believers, children of the same Father: "Christian brotherhood is ultimately founded on the faith that gives us our assurance of our real sonship in relation to the heavenly Father and of our brotherhood among one another."[122] Ratzinger illustrates this dimension of essential fraternity in a reflection on the same Father.[123] He notes that contemporary theologians often explicate the Our Father with an analysis of just the word "Father," unlike the Church Fathers—for example, St. Cyprian—for whom reflection on the word "our" was of great importance: "For 'me' he becomes a Father

---

[118] Ratzinger, *Faith and the Future*, 44.

[119] Ratzinger et al., *Handing on the Faith*, 27.

[120] Ratzinger, *To Look on Christ*, 37.

[121] Ratzinger, *To Look on Christ*, 30.

[122] Joseph Ratzinger, *The Meaning of Christian Brotherhood* (San Francisco: Ignatius Press, 1993), 51.

[123] Joseph Ratzinger, *The Meaning of Christian Brotherhood*, 51–52.

only through my being in the 'we' of his children."[124] The Our Father "is not the call of a soul that knows nothing outside God and itself"[125]; it is the prayer that the "we" can only truly pray *in* community. For this reason, authentic faith is always ecclesial:

> What is essential is that I cannot build my personal faith in a private dialogue with Jesus. Faith lives in this "we," or else it is not alive. Faith and life, truth and life, "I" and "we," are not divisible, and it is only in the context of sharing in the life of the "we" who believe, the "we" of the Church, that faith develops its logic, its organic shape.[126]

The organic and complete faith is one that is lived as an ecclesial act. That is why "the act of faith is always an act of becoming a participant in a totality; it is an act of *communio*, a willingness to be incorporated into the communion of witnesses, so that we with them and in them may touch the untouchable, hear the inaudible, and see the invisible."[127] Believing is always an act of communion; it implies trust in what others communicate to us, the acceptance of what we have not seen firsthand, and the consciousness of our essential fraternity. For the same reasons, believing means "letting ourselves be torn away from

---

[124] Joseph Ratzinger, *The Meaning of Christian Brotherhood*, 51

[125] Joseph Ratzinger, *Volk und Haus Gottes in Augustins Lehre von der Kirche* (Munich: Karl Zink, 1954), 99, cited in Ratzinger, *The Meaning of Christian Brotherhood*, 51.

[126] Ratzinger, *To Look on Christ*, 38.

[127] Ratzinger et al., *Handing on the Faith*, 28.

the selfishness of someone who is living only for himself and entering into the great basic orientation of existing for the sake of another."[128] Through the faith that we receive through Baptism "we lose ourselves as a separate, independent 'I' and find ourselves again in the new 'I.'"[129] This renunciation of a solitary and self-sufficient "I" is the door to a faith that is shared among believers. Thus we can see the hopeful truth that "faith confers community [and] vanquishes loneliness. He who believes is not alone."[130] In a very simple way, we can say that we are not sufficient unto ourselves, that we need the company of others who take us to encounter the Lord. Ratzinger said this beautifully in a homily back in 1964:

> It is at this point that faith begins. For what faith basically means is just that this shortfall that we all have in our love is made up by the surplus of Jesus Christ's love, acting on our behalf. He simply tells us that God himself has poured out among us a superabundance of his love and has thus made good in advance all our deficiency. Ultimately, faith means nothing other than admitting that we have this kind of shortfall; it means opening our hand and accepting a gift. In its simplest and innermost form, faith is nothing but reaching that point in love at which we recognize that we, too, need to be given

---

[128] Ratzinger, *What It Means to Be a Christian*, 57.

[129] Ratzinger, *Principles of Catholic Theology*, 33.

[130] Ratzinger, *Principles of Catholic Theology*, 83.

something. Faith is thus that stage in love in overcoming the complacency and self-satisfaction of the person who says "I have done everything, I don't need any further help." It is only in "faith" like this that selfishness, the real opposite of love, comes to an end. To that extent, faith is already present in and with true loving; it simply represents that impulse in love which leads to its finding its true self: the openness of someone who does not insist on his own capabilities, but is aware of receiving something as a gift and standing in need of it.[131]

Only in the Church can we find this true love that faith demands. In her we learn to believe, to welcome others, to help each other, to deepen our faith, to understand it, pray, and live it, and to worship and adore God: "Thus belief embraces, as essential parts of itself, the profession of faith, the word, and the unity it effects; it embraces entry into the community's worship of God and, so, finally the fellowship we call Church."[132]

It is in the liturgy of the Church that this unity finds its source and summit. The act of worshipping God according to the universality proper to authentic Christian liturgy, in true openness to all mankind and all history, gives the foundation for a true Catholic communion.[133] In the act of conforming ourselves

---

[131] Ratzinger, *What It Means to Be a Christian*, 74–75.

[132] Ratzinger, *Introduction to Christianity*, 100.

[133] See Ratzinger, *The Spirit of the Liturgy*, in Ratzinger, *Collected Works*, 11:30.

to Jesus' own prayer, that is, the *Logike latreia* (the worship according to the *Logos*), according to the liturgical acts and prayers of the Church, are believers given the "logic," the right "grammar," the "speech" that allows them the freedom of praying with the language of Mother Church:

> The language of our Mother becomes ours; we learn to speak it along with her, so that gradually, her words on our lips become our words. We are given an anticipatory share in the Church's perennial dialogue of love with him who desired to be one flesh with her, and this gift is transformed into the gift of speech. And it is in the gift of speech, and not until then, that I am really restored to my true self; only thus am I given back to God, handed over by him to all my fellow men; only thus am I free.[134]

The Church is an environment of unity of faith, in which the "I" of the believer is converted from a private to an ecclesial "I."[135] Indeed, "this 'I' utters itself only in the *communio* of the Church."[136] In this *communio*, the unity of faith comes to fruition, above all as unity among believers. Faith in its most constructive essence "unites subject and object but even brings individual subjects together without depriv-

---

[134] Ratzinger, *The Feast of Faith*, 30.

[135] Ratzinger, *Principles of Catholic Theology*, 23.

[136] Ratzinger, *Principles of Catholic Theology*, 23.

ing them of their individuality."[137] This unity of faith also signifies that the natural separation of time is overcome; faith "links people not only right across frontiers of language and race, but also across thousands of years."[138] This is done in particular through the memory of the Church, as a mediation between being and time: "The seat of all faith is, then, the *memoria Ecclesiae*, the memory of the Church, the Church as memory. It exists through all ages, waxing and waning but never ceasing to be the common *situs* [place] of faith."[139] In the Church we have one faith: "[W]ithout this [believing] subject, which unifies the whole, the content of faith is neither more nor less than a long catalogue of things to be believed; within and by the Church, they are made one."[140]

The faith as an ecclesial act, and therefore an act

---

[137] Ratzinger, *Principles of Catholic Theology*, 26

[138] Ratzinger, *Faith and the Future*, 37.

[139] Ratzinger, *Principles of Catholic Theology*, 23.

[140] Ratzinger, *Principles of Catholic Theology*, 23–24. Maximilian Heim summarizes this aspect of Ratzinger's theology with these words: "For Ratzinger, the Church is the transtemporal subject of faith that is rooted in the trinitarian mystery and testifies to its identity along with its origin in Christ. As such, the Church is and professes the unity of believers from the various eras over the course of history. For this reason, she is also 'the condition for the real participation in Jesus' *traditio*, which without the subject exists, not as a historical and history-making reality, but only as a private recollection.' Therefore the individual always believes by believing along with the whole Church" (Maximilian Heinrich Heim, *Joseph Ratzinger: Life in the Church and Living Theology* [San Francisco: Ignatius Press, 2007], 149).

made as members of one body and one history, is understood as "the one road by which men can travel to God."[141] For this way to be most effective and to bring us closer to God, it is necessary that there be a vital testimony that convinces not only with words, but with life: "The courage to believe cannot be communicated today, as formerly, in a purely intellectual manner. It requires first and foremost witnesses who verify faith as the correct path through their living and their suffering."[142] Coherence is the decisive criterion for the presentation of the faith. What is really important is not the numbers, the data, or the majorities, but the quality of the faith as it is lived. And here we are able to understand yet again the importance of the saints. In the lives of the saints we find the criterion for learning to believe. Indeed, "the fortuitous majorities that may form here or there in the Church do not decide their and our path: they, the saints, are the true, the normative majority by which we orient ourselves."[143] In the saints we find the consolation of being accompanied in our journey of faith. In faith, we live with them, they speak to us and understand us as we understand them.[144] With them we say, "I believe you, Christ, who rose from the dead. I hold fast to you. I do not come alone in the mortal loneliness of those who cannot love. I come in the communion of saints, who even in death do not leave me."[145]

---

[141] Ratzinger, *Faith and the Future*, 37.

[142] Ratzinger, *A Turning Point for Europe?*, 109.

[143] Ratzinger, *Called to Communion*, 154.

[144] See Ratzinger, *Principles of Catholic Theology*, 83.

[145] Joseph Ratzinger, *Images of Hope: Meditations on Major Feasts*, trans. John Rock and Graham Harrison (San Fran-

According to the saints, faith is also understood as an ecclesial mission: to proclaim, with word and testimony, what we have received as a gift. In a world that believes less and less, this mission could be seen by pessimists as a fruitless endeavor. The world, however, truly needs the Christian faith: "The missionary tendency of this faith is based on that claim: Only if the Christian faith is truth does it concern all men,"[146] and indeed, Christianity "claims to tell us the truth about God, the world, and man."[147] The Christian faith has something essential to say today, because it responds to the nature of the human being, since it comes from God. The Christian faith as an ecclesial act is an intrinsically missionary act. Proclaiming the Good News and giving testimony are part of the believer's pilgrimage of faith.

Faith is an ecclesial act. In this "pilgrim fellowship of the Church,"[148] we travel along the path of faith, which is the road that calls for a permanent effort of conversion, of opening up to the *Logos* that has become flesh in Jesus of Nazareth, with whom we are called to conform our lives. Faith is conversion,[149] knowledge and praxis,[150] trust and joy,[151] the way[152] founded on the truth: it is "truth as a way that makes

---

cisco: Ignatius Press, 2006), 99.
[146] Ratzinger, *Truth and Tolerance*, 184.
[147] Ratzinger, *Truth and Tolerance*, 184.
[148] Ratzinger, *Pilgrim Fellowship of Faith*, 6.
[149] Ratzinger, *Principles of Catholic Theology*, 55–60.
[150] Ratzinger, *Principles of Catholic Theology*, 67–75.
[151] Ratzinger, *Principles of Catholic Theology*, 75–84.
[152] Ratzinger, *La Fe como camino*, 55.

a claim upon [us], that [we] can and must tread."[153] Faith is not a cold collection of facts, nor an empty vacuum of habits; it is the truth that we embrace, in which we live; it is, in the last instance, Christ Himself, who "called himself truth, not custom."[154]

---

[153] Ratzinger, *Introduction to Christianity*, 100.

[154] "Dominus noster Christus veritatem se, non consuetudinem cognominavit" (Tertullian, *De virginibus velandis* I, cited in Ratzinger, *Introduction to Christianity*, 141).

Afterword

Having reflected on the act of believing according to the thought of Joseph Ratzinger, it is my hope that, amid the several different insights and topics mentioned, a meaningful vision of the act of faith can be grasped.

This vision is relevant. Not only because Ratzinger's insights are profound and fascinating but because they offer a true contribution to the conversation about faith in our world today. This contribution is valuable not only for academics, but for anyone who faces the challenge of faith: for believers, for those who doubt, and for unbelievers. This rich vision of faith as a gift and as an act is more necessary than ever in our times: the crisis of the Church is a crisis of faith; the renewal of the Church has to begin with a renewal of faith. A deep, robust, and relatable understanding of what it means to believe is, truly, an urgent and necessary task for the Church, and this is precisely what Ratzinger offers us in his writings.

However, in the end, more than just reading "professional theology," we have joined the journey of faith of a believer who unites in a unique way the knowledge and intellectual experience of decades of study and teaching with years of humble prayer and service—a path of faith that has certainly not always been easy.

Only five days before departing the Vatican to begin his life of silence and prayer as Pope Emeritus, at the end of the spiritual exercises with the Roman Curia, Benedict XVI said: "To believe is none other than, in the obscurity of the world, to touch the hand of God and thus, in silence, to hear the Word, to see Love."[1] These words suffice to close this short volume. In them we feel the depth of a long life of believing, of learning and teaching about the faith, and of trusting in the love of Christ in the midst of obscure moments. These words, spoken by a man of faith, are like a threshold into the stillness of a life that will remain in the mystery of God's hiddenness. We can only be grateful for what Joseph Ratzinger has taught us about what is means to believe, and pray that, from the silence in which he dwells, he can hear the Word and see Love.

---

[1] Benedict XVI, Address at the Conclusion of the Week of Spiritual Exercises for the Roman Curia, February 23, 2013 (available at http://www.vatican.va/content/benedict-xvi/en/speeches/2013/february/documents/hf_ben-xvi_spe_20130223_esercizi-spirituali.html).

Bibliography

Ratzinger, Joseph. *A New Song for the Lord: Faith in Christ and Liturgy Today.* Translated by Martha M. Matesich. New York: Crossroad, 1997.

———. *A Turning Point for Europe? The Church in the Modern World: Assessment and Forecast.* Translated by Brian McNeil, CRV. San Francisco: Ignatius Press, 2010.

———. *Al Servicio del Evangelio.* Lima: Vida y Espiritualidad, 2003.

———. *Called to Communion: Understanding the Church Today.* Translated by Adrian Walker. San Francisco: Ignatius Press, 1991.

———. *Christianity and the Crisis of Cultures.* Translated by Brian McNeil. San Francisco: Ignatius Press, 2006.

———. *Collected Works: Theology of the Liturgy.* Edited by Michael J. Miller. San Francisco: Ignatius Press, 2014.

———. *Dogma and Preaching: Applying Christian Doctrine to Daily Life.* Translated by Michael J. Miller and Matthew J. O'Connell. San Francisco: Ignatius Press, 2011.

———. *Einführung in das Christentum.* Munich: Kösel-Verlag, 1968.

———. *El Dios de la fe y el Dios de los filósofos.* Madrid: Taurus, 1960.

———. *Eschatology: Death and Eternal Life.* Translated by Michael Waldstein. Washington, DC: The Catholic University of America Press, 1988.

———. "Europe in the Crisis of Cultures." *Communio* 32 (Summer 2005): 351. https://www.theway.org.uk/endeanweb/ratzinger32-2.pdf.

———. *Europe: Today and Tomorrow.* Translated by Michael J. Miller. San Francisco: Ignatius Press, 2007.

———. *Faith and the Future.* San Francisco: Ignatius Press, 2009.

———. *God and the World: A Conversation with Peter Seewald.* Translated by Henry Taylor. San Francisco: Ignatius Press, 2002.

———. *God Is Near Us: The Eucharist, the Heart of Life*. Translated by Henry Taylor. San Francisco: Ignatius Press, 2003.

———. *Gospel, Catechesis, Catechism: Sidelights on the Catechism of the Catholic Church*. Translated by Adrian Walker. San Francisco: Ignatius Press, 1997.

———. Homily at the Mass "Pro Eligendo Romano Pontifice." April 18, 2005. Available at http://www.vatican.va/gpII/documents/homily-pro-eligendo-pontifice_20050418_en.html.

———. *Images of Hope: Meditations on Major Feasts*. Translated by John Rock and Graham Harrison. San Francisco: Ignatius Press, 2006.

———. *In the Beginning: A Catholic Understanding of the Story of Creation and the Fall*. Translated by Boniface Ramsey, OP. Grand Rapids, MI: Eerdmans, 1995.

———. *Introduction to Christianity*. Translated by J. R. Foster. San Francisco: Ignatius Press, 2004.

———. *La Fe como camino: Contribución al ethos cristiano en el momento actual*. Barcelona: Ediciones Internacionales Universitarias, 1997.

———. *Many Religions—One Covenant: Israel, the Church and the World*. Translated by Graham Harrison. San Francisco: Ignatius Press, 1999.

———. *On the Way to Jesus Christ*. Translated by Michael J. Miller. San Francisco: Ignatius Press, 2005.

———. *Pilgrim Fellowship of Faith: The Church as Communion*. Translated by Henry Taylor. San Francisco: Ignatius Press, 2005.

———. *Principles of Catholic Theology: Building Stones for a Fundamental Theology*. Translated by Sister Mary Frances McCarthy, SND. San Francisco: Ignatius Press, 1987.

———. "Reviving the Tradition: Concerning the Notion of Person in Theology." *Communio* 17 (Fall 1990): 447.

———. *Salt of the Earth: The Church at the End of the Millennium: An Interview with Peter Seewald*. Translated by Adrian Walker. San Francisco: Ignatius Press, 1997.

———. *Ser Cristiano en la Era Neopagana*. Madrid: Encuentro, 1995.

———. *Storia e dogma* [History and dogma]. Milan: Jaca Book, 1993.

———. *The Feast of Faith: Approaches to a Theology of the Liturgy*. Translated by Graham Harrison. San Francisco: Ignatius Press, 1986.

———. *The God of Jesus Christ: Meditations on the Triune God*. Translated by Brian McNeil. San Francisco: Ignatius Press, 2008.

———. *The Meaning of Christian Brotherhood*. San Francisco: Ignatius Press, 1993.

———. *The Spirit of the Liturgy*. Translated by John Saward. San Francisco: Ignatius Press, 2000.

———. "The Theology of the Liturgy." In Joseph Ratzinger et al., *Looking Again at the Question of the Liturgy with Cardinal Ratzinger*. Edited by Alcuin Reid. Farnborough: Saint Michael's Abbey Press, 2003.

———. "Thoughts on the Place of Marian Doctrine and Piety in Faith and Theology as a Whole." In Joseph Ratzinger and Hans Urs von Balthasar, *Mary: The Church at the Source*. San Francisco: Ignatius Press, 2005.

———. *To Look on Christ: Exercises in Faith, Hope, and Love*. Translated by Robert Nowell. New York: Crossroad, 1991.

———. *Truth and Tolerance: Christian Belief and World Religions*. Translated by Henry Taylor. San Francisco: Ignatius Press, 2004.

———. *Values in a Time of Upheaval*. Translated by Brian McNeil. New York: Crossroad, 2006.

———. *What It Means to Be a Christian: Three Sermons*. Translated by Henry Taylor. San Francisco: Ignatius Press, 2006.

Ratzinger, Joseph, Godfried Daneels, Franciszek Macharski, and Dermot Ryan. *Handing on the Faith in an Age of Disbelief.* Translated by Michael J. Miller. San Francisco: Ignatius Press, 2006.

SECONDARY SOURCES

———. *Joseph Ratzinger: Razón y cristianismo: La Victoria de la inteligencia en el mundo de las religiones* [Reason and Christianity: The victory of the intelligence in the world of religions]. Madrid: Rialp, 2005.

———. "*Logos* and *Dia-Logos*: Faith, Reason, (and Love) According to Joseph Ratzinger." *Anglican Theological Review* 92, no. 3 (2010). http://www.anglicantheologicalreview.org/static/pdf/articles/sarto.pdf

Crean, Thomas. *God Is No Delusion: A Refutation of Richard Dawkins.* San Francisco: Ignatius, 2007.

De Gaál, Emery. *The Theology of Pope Benedict XVI: The Christocentric Shift.* New York: Palgrave Macmillan, 2010.

Guerriero, Elio. *Benedict XVI: His Life and Thought.* Translated by William J. Melcher. San Francisco: Ignatius Press, 2018.

Harrison, Carol. *The Art of Listening in the Early Church.* Oxford: Oxford University Press, 2013.

Hart, David Bentley. *Atheist Delusions: The Christian Revolution and Its Fashionable Enemies*. New Haven: Yale University Press, 2009.

Heim, Maximilian Heinrich. *Joseph Ratzinger: Life in the Church and Living Theology*. San Francisco: Ignatius Press, 2007.

Murphy, Joseph. *Christ Our Joy: The Theological Vision of Pope Benedict XVI*. San Francisco: Ignatius Press, 2008.

Newman, John Henry. *Apologia pro Vita Sua: Being a History of His Religious Opinions*. London: Longmans, Green, Reader, and Dyer, 1875.

Nichols, Aidan. *The Thought of Benedict XVI: An Introduction to the Theology of Joseph Ratzinger*. London: Burns & Oates, 2005.

Rowland, Tracey. *Ratzinger's Faith: The Theology of Pope Benedict XVI*. Oxford: Oxford University Press, 2008.

Sarto, Pablo Blanco. *Joseph Ratzinger: Una Biografía*. Pamplona: Eunsa, 2004

Seewald, Peter. *Benedict XVI: An Intimate Portrait*. Translated by Henry Taylor and Anne Englund Nash. San Francisco: Ignatius Press, 2008.

Twomey, Vincent. *Benedict XVI: The Conscience of Our Age: A Theological Portrait*. San Francisco: Ignatius Press, 2007.

OTHER WORKS

A Greek-English Lexicon. Edited by Henry George Liddell and Robert Scott. Oxford: Oxford University Press, 1990.

A Greek-English Lexicon of the New Testament and Other Early Christian Literature. A translation and adaptation of Walter Bauer's Griechisch-Deutsches Wörterbuch zu den Schriften des Neuen Testaments und der übrigen urchristlichen Literatur. Fourth revised and augmented edition. Translated and edited by William F. Arndt and F. Wilbur Gingrich. Cambridge and Chicago: Cambridge University Press and The University of Chicago Press, 1957.

Index

Activism, 78
Agnosticism, 26, 28–30, 33, 35–36
Aquinas, Thomas (saint), 77, 85
Aristotle, 24
assent, 77
    of faith, 78, 83
    to God, 42, 82
atheism, 27
    "new atheism", 27n42
    scientific, 28
Augustine, Saint, 7, 72

Being, 16, 37, 40, 45, 53–54, 56, 68–70, 85, 91, 96
Being and time, 95
    Being and truth, 24
    Being itself, 26
    created, 61
    God's being, 55–56
    human, xiii, 23, 36, 47–48, 51, 74, 76, 79, 97
    of the believer, 63, 69
    our, 53, 68, 70, 85
belief, 15, 41, 43–45, 50, 57, 64, 70, 79, 83, 86, 89, 90, 93
    "Belief in the World of Today," 14

　　　　　and uncertainty, 16, 19
　　　　　challenge of, 14
　　　　　Christian, 44, 49
　　　　　problem of, 17
believe, to, 3–5, 7–8, 12, 14–18, 18n14, 28, 31, 33–39, 41–45, 47–50, 53, 55–61, 68–69, 77–79, 82–83, 85–93, 95, 95n140, 96–97, 99–100
believer, 6, 16–18, 40
Benedict (saint), 2
Blanco, Pablo, 36n1, 41n16, 59

Church Fathers, 2, 10–11, 37, 90
Church, the, 3, 5–6, 9, 53, 67, 76, 89–91, 93–95, 95n140, 96. *See also* ecclesia
　　　　　and Mary, 76
　　　　　Body, 67
　　　　　Catechism, 65
　　　　　Christ in the Church, 11
　　　　　community, 53, 94
　　　　　crisis, 99
　　　　　early Church, 10
　　　　　faith, 33
　　　　　fellowship, 97
　　　　　in the twentieth and twenty-first centuries, 3
　　　　　liturgy, 93
　　　　　memory, 95
　　　　　as Mother, 94
　　　　　prayers, 94
　　　　　renewal, 99
　　　　　task, 6, 99
　　　　　today, 3, 6
Claudel, Paul, 16
Contemporary theology, 21

conversion, 10, 18n14, 38, 40, 44, 45, 47, 51, 53, 62, 66, 97. *See also* metanoia
Creed, 14–15, 86, 88
    Anglican, 18n14
    Christian, 18n14
    contents, 58
    of the Church, 32
    Ratzinger's commentary, 14
    text, 45
crisis, 5, 19, 21, 99
culture, 3, 26–27, 29, 72
Cyprian (saint), 90

Descartes, 24–25
dialogue, 12, 68, 86
    act of, 88
    fruit of, 33, 87
    perennial, 94
    private, 91
doubt, 4–5, 16–18, 18n14, 19–20, 75, 99
    and belief, 17
    and faith, 14
    form of, 17
    the term, 16n5

ecclesia, 8, 91. *See also* Church
    "I", 94
    ecclesial aspect, 86
    ecclesial dimension, 86, 90
    ecclesial act, 53, 85, 91, 95, 97
    memoria ecclesiae, 95
    ecclesial mission, 97
epistemology, 32

evidence, 56, 77, 84
existence, 17, 29, 38, 40–41, 45–46, 48, 57, 63, 68, 70, 72, 88
- Christian, 6
- of truth, 31, 33
- coexistence between science and religion, 74

experience, 1, 3–4, 10–11, 17, 20, 23, 39, 56, 60, 63 66, 68, 78–81, 84–86, 89, 100
- of faith, 14, 18n14, 54, 66, 79, 81, 85
- of love, 62, 68
- of uncertainty, 15–16, 20

fact, 14, 18n14, 24–25, 49, 61–62, 66, 76, 81–82, 84, 98
- *factum*, 24, 76

faith, 1, 3–7, 9, 11–18, 18n14, 19–21, 21n18, 22–23, 26–29, 31–33, 35–36, 37–40, 42–50, 54–68, 70–99
- and daily life, 6, 11, 20, 39, 40, 78
- and the Church, 91–95, 97, 99
- as a challenge, 4, 15, 35, 99
- as a gift, 8, 36–38, 47, 50, 53–54, 56, 62, 64, 69, 79, 99
- as an act, 7, 15, 19, 36, 38, 45–46, 51, 64–66, 68–69, 77–79, 81–82, 84, 89, 91, 95, 97, 99
- as encounter, 61–63, 65
- as trust, 33, 38–40, 43–44, 46, 48–49, 57–58, 66–67, 76, 83, 91, 97
- as understanding, 47, 49–50, 57
- integral: mind, heart, will, 69–70, 79

freedom, 46, 62, 64–65, 67–68, 79, 94
- and relativism, 30, 32

friendship, 4
- with Jesus Christ, 53–54, 62, 66–68, 76

Functional Rationality, 27

Guardini, Romano, 3, 17

Harrison, Carol, 10
Heisenberg, Werner, 75
Historicism, 24–25
hope, 6, 31, 45, 57, 82

identity, 53, 63, 90, 95n140
insecurity, 15–17, 18n14

Jesus, 1, 4, 7, 33, 53–57, 61, 63, 66–68, 80, 82–85, 90, 92, 94–95
    as Logos, 58–59, 73
justice, 31

Kant, Immanuel, 24
knowledge, 6, 24–26, 38–40, 48, 50, 71–72, 75–76, 79–80, 82, 100
    and faith, 23, 54, 69, 76, 97
    and friendship with Christ, 62, 66–67
    of faith, 79–82, 84
    of God, 4, 36–37, 80, 84

liturgy, 93
    baptismal, 86
Logos, 48, 58–61, 65, 73, 82, 84, 94
love, 59, 61, 64–65, 68, 70, 84, 92, 94, 96
    in faith, 57, 58, 61–62, 64, 66, 70, 77, 92–93
    in Jesus and the Trinity, 60–61, 63–64, 67, 69, 73, 76, 81, 82–83, 92, 100

of Jesus Christ and God, 3–4, 11, 66, 68

Marx, Karl, 24, 47
Mary, 78
meaning, 35–38, 42, 45, 48–51, 54, 56–57, 59–60, 63, 73–74, 76–77, 82, 84
metanoia, 45, 62. *See also* conversion
mission, 56, 97
modernity, 14n2, 20, 23, 26
Moses, 55
mystery, 44, 47, 49–50, 61, 80, 100
    of Benedict XVI's pontificate, 3
    of the Trinity, 95

Newman, John Henry (saint), 18n14
Nihilism, 16, 31, 33

obedience, 68

Patristics, 10
peace, 2, 22, 31, 79
person, 2, 17, 18n14, 29, 34, 44, 54, 66, 74, 79, 82, 88, 93
    God as personal, 55–57, 82
    modern, 32
    Persons of the Trinity, 45, 81
    personal opinions, 34
    interpersonal relationships, 34
    personal identities, 51
    knowledge, 82
    of Jesus Christ, 4, 33, 54, 56, 59–63, 82–83,
    personal nature of faith, 8, 44, 47, 51, 53–56, 58, 63, 65, 69–70, 76, 79, 85–87, 90–91

of Patristic theology, 10, 11
philosophy, 21, 73, 87
Planck, Max, 74, 74n67

reality, 6, 16, 22–23, 25–26, 28–29, 40–42, 49–51, 59–61, 63–64, 68, 73, 80, 83
    of faith, 6, 19, 35, 40, 70, 84, 95
reason, 5, 8–9, 12–13, 22, 41, 49, 59–62, 70–71, 73–78, 83, 91, 95n140
    and faith, 49–50, 71, 73–74, 76
    divine, 50, 81–82
    natural, 36
    positive, 25
    sentiment, and will, 69, 75–79
relationship, 34, 37, 47, 60, 68, 77,
    with Jesus Christ and God, 53–54, 56–57, 66, 68, 84, 89
relativism, 20, 30–36
    religious, 72
religion, 18n14, 22, 27n42, 55, 71–76
    new, 32
    of reason, 71
    sources of religion, 72
    true, 73
    world, 71
revelation, 44, 57,
    divine, 37, 84
    as in Scripture, 18n14
    God's, 12–13

saints, 10, 85, 96–97
Schleiermacher, Friedrich, 75, 75n69
science, 22, 28–29, 74–75, 77, 82

    natural, 26, 49
    of faith, 85
Scientific Method, 25–26, 30, 32, 36
Seewald, Peter, 17
sentiment and sentimentality, 22, 69, 74–79

The Trinity, 45, 81
Thérèse of Lisieux (saint), 15
tolerance, 32–34
trust, 7, 15, 33–34, 38–40, 42–44, 46–49, 56–57, 66–67, 76, 83, 97, 100
    and belief, 15–16, 18, 39, 43, 48–49, 57–58, 91, 100
truth, 12, 16, 24–26, 30–34, 37, 42, 47, 49–50, 54, 59, 60–62, 71–74, 76, 82, 86, 89, 91–92, 97–98
    and being, 24,
    and love, 60–61, 73, 76, 77, 82
    revealed, 18n14, 74

unbelief, 15–16, 18–19, 36
unbeliever/-s, 16–18, 74
uncertainty, 15–17, 19, 31
understanding, 23, 25, 32, 48, 51, 59, 70, 75, 77–79
    and faith, 6, 14, 20, 47, 49–50, 57, 71

Vico, Giambattista, 24, 47